AQA Mathematics

Unit 1 · Foundation

New GCSE

Series Editor
Paul Metcalf

Series Advisor
Andy Darbourne

Lead Authors
Sandra Burns
Shaun Procter-Green
Margaret Thornton

Authors
Tony Fisher
June Haighton
Anne Haworth
Gill Hewlett
Andrew Manning
Ginette McManus
Howard Prior
David Pritchard
Dave Ridgway
Paul Winters

Nelson Thornes

Published in 2010 by:
Nelson Thornes Ltd
Delta Place
27 Bath Road
CHELTENHAM
GL53 7TH
United Kingdom

10 11 12 13 14 / 10 9 8 7 6 5 4 3 2 1

A catalogue record for this book is available from the British Library

ISBN 978 1 4085 0621 9

Cover photograph: iStockphoto
Illustrations by Rupert Besley, Roger Penwill and Tech-Set Limited
Page make-up by Tech-Set Limited, Gateshead

Printed and bound in Spain by GraphyCems

Photograph acknowledgements
Alamy: Alex Segre / 7.16; **Fotolia:** 1.4; 5.1; C1.3; 9.7;
Getty Images: AFP / 2.1; 2.4; 3.4; C.1.2; **iStockphoto:** 1.1; 2.7; 3.1; 4.10; 5.6; 8.1;
9.5; **NASA:** 5.9.

Contents

Introduction   5

Chapter 1 Fractions   7

1.1 Integers   8
1.2 Multiplying and dividing positive
      and negative integers   10
1.3 Fractions   12
1.4 Equivalent fractions   14
1.5 Arranging fractions in order   17
1.6 Fractions of quantities   18
1.7 One quantity as a fraction of another   19
     Chapter 1 Assess   21

Chapter 2 Decimals   23

2.1 Place value   24
2.2 Rounding   25
2.3 Adding and subtracting decimals   26
2.4 Multiplying decimals   28
2.5 Fractions and decimals   29
     Chapter 2 Assess   30

Chapter 3 Collecting data   32

3.1 Types of data   33
3.2 Data collection methods   36
3.3 Organising data   39
     Chapter 3 Assess   43

Chapter 4 Percentages   46

4.1 Percentages, fractions and decimals   47
4.2 Finding a percentage of a quantity   49
4.3 Increasing or decreasing by a percentage   51
4.4 Writing one quantity as a percentage of another   54
4.5 Percentage increase and decrease   57
     Chapter 4 Assess   59

Chapter 5 Ratio and proportion — 61

5.1	Finding and simplifying ratios	62
5.2	Using ratios to find quantities	64
5.3	Ratio and proportion: the unitary method	66
	Chapter 5 Assess	69

Chapter 6 Statistical measures — 71

6.1	Basic measures	72
6.2	Frequency distributions	74
6.3	Grouped frequency distributions	78
	Chapter 6 Assess	81

Chapter 7 Representing data — 83

7.1	Pictograms, bar charts and pie charts	84
7.2	Stem-and-leaf diagrams	89
7.3	Line graphs, frequency polygons and histograms	92
	Chapter 7 Assess	96

Chapter 8 Scatter graphs — 99

8.1	Plotting points on a scatter graph	100
8.2	Interpreting scatter graphs	103
8.3	Lines of best fit	107
	Chapter 8 Assess	110

Chapter 9 Probability — 112

9.1	Describing probability	113
9.2	Combining events	116
9.3	Mutually exclusive events	118
9.4	Relative frequency	121
	Chapter 9 Assess	125

Consolidation — 127

| Glossary | 137 |
| Index | 140 |

Nelson Thornes and AQA

Nelson Thornes has worked in partnership with AQA to ensure that this book and the accompanying online resources offer you the best support for your GCSE course.

All AQA endorsed resources undergo a thorough quality assurance process to ensure that their contents closely match the AQA specification. You can be confident that the content of materials branded with AQA's 'Exclusively Endorsed' logo have been written, checked and approved by AQA senior examiners, in order to achieve AQA's exclusive endorsement.

The print and online resources together unlock blended learning; this means that the links between the activities in the book and the activities online blend together to maximise your understanding of a topic and help you achieve your potential.

These online resources are available on *kerboodle!* which can be accessed via the internet at **www.kerboodle.com/live**, anytime, anywhere.

If your school or college subscribes to *kerboodle!* you will be provided with your own personal login details. Once logged in, access your course and locate the required activity.

For more information and help on how to use visit **www.kerboodle.com**.

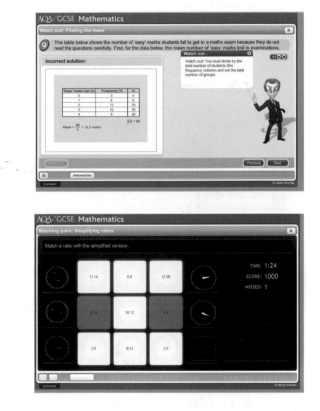

How to use this book

To help you unlock blended learning, we have referenced the activities in this book that have additional online coverage in *kerboodle!* by using this icon:

The icons in this book show you the online resources available from the start of the new specification and will always be relevant.

In addition, to keep the blend up-to-date and engaging, we review customer feedback and may add new content onto *kerboodle!* after publication!

Welcome to GCSE Mathematics

This book has been written by teachers and examiners who not only want you to get the best grade you can in your GCSE exam, but also to enjoy maths. It covers all the material you will need to know for AQA GCSE Mathematics Unit 1 Foundation. This unit allows you to use a calculator, so you will be able to use this most of the time throughout this book. Look out for calculator or non-calculator symbols (shown below) which tell you whether to use a calculator or not.

In the exam, you will be tested on the Assessment Objectives (AOs) below. Ask your teacher if you need help to understand what these mean.

AO1 recall and use your knowledge of the prescribed content

AO2 select and apply mathematical methods in a range of contexts

AO3 interpret and analyse problems and generate strategies to solve them.

Each chapter is made up of the following features:

Objectives

The objectives at the start of the chapter give you an idea of what you need to do to get each grade. Remember that the examiners expect you to do well at the lower grade questions on the exam paper in order to get the higher grades. So, even if you are aiming for a Grade C you will still need to do well on the Grade G questions on the exam paper.

On the first page of every chapter, there are also words that you will need to know or understand, called Key Terms. The box called 'You should already know' describes the maths that you will have learned before studying this chapter. There is also an interesting fact at the beginning of each chapter which tells you about maths in real life.

 Learn...

The Learn sections give you the key information and examples to show how to do each topic. There are several Learn sections in each chapter.

Practise...

Questions that allow you to practise what you have just learned.

E The bars that run alongside questions in the exercises show you what grade the question is aimed at. This will give you an idea of what grade you're working at. Don't forget, even if you are aiming at a Grade C, you will still need to do well on the Grades G–D questions.

  These questions are Functional Maths type questions, which show how maths can be used in real life.

? These questions are problem solving questions, which will require you to think carefully about how best to answer.

⚠ These questions are harder questions.

▦ These questions should be attempted **with** a calculator.

⊠ These questions should be attempted **without** using a calculator.

Assess

End of chapter questions written by examiners. Some chapters feature additional questions taken from real past papers to further your understanding.

Hint

These are tips for you to remember whilst learning the maths or answering questions.

AQA Examiner's tip

These are tips from the people who will mark your exams, giving you advice on things to remember and watch out for.

Bump up your grade

These are tips from the people who will mark your exams, giving you help on how to boost your grade, especially aimed at getting a Grade C.

Consolidation

The consolidation chapter allows you to practise what you have learned in previous chapters. The questions in these chapters can cover any of the topics you have already seen.

1 Fractions

Objectives

Examiners would normally expect students who get these grades to be able to:

G

understand positive and negative integers

find which fraction of a shape is shaded

put integers and simple fractions in order

express simple decimals and percentages as fractions

find equivalent fractions

F

add and subtract negative numbers

calculate fractions of quantities

simplify fractions

arrange fractions in order

E

multiply and divide negative numbers

express fractions as decimals and percentages

add and subtract fractions

D

find one quantity as a fraction of another

solve problems involving fractions

C

add and subtract mixed numbers.

Did you know?

Fractions in music

In a lot of music the strongest beats happen at regular intervals. This divides the music up into 'bars'. Each bar takes the same time to play. Most bars have several notes in them, so the notes are fractions of a bar. The notes in a bar can vary in length, some are longer and some are shorter. However, they always have to add up to the length of the bar. So musicians keep in time with each other by adding up fractions!

Key terms

integer
positive number
negative number
natural (counting) number
directed number

mixed number
equivalent fractions
numerator
denominator

You should already know:

✔ how to add, subtract, multiply and divide simple numbers

✔ the meaning of 'sum', 'difference' and 'product'

✔ simple fractions such as halves and quarters.

Learn... 1.1 Integers

Integers are whole numbers, such as 3, −4, +55, −256, 0

An integer can be a **positive number**, a **negative number** or zero. The positive integers 1, 2, 3, and so on are also called the **natural** or **counting numbers**.

A negative (−) sign is always used to show that an integer is less than zero.

A positive (+) sign can be used to show that an integer is greater than zero.

Numbers with either positive or negative signs are called **directed numbers**.

A number line is useful for arranging integers in order and adding and subtracting.

Arranging directed numbers in order

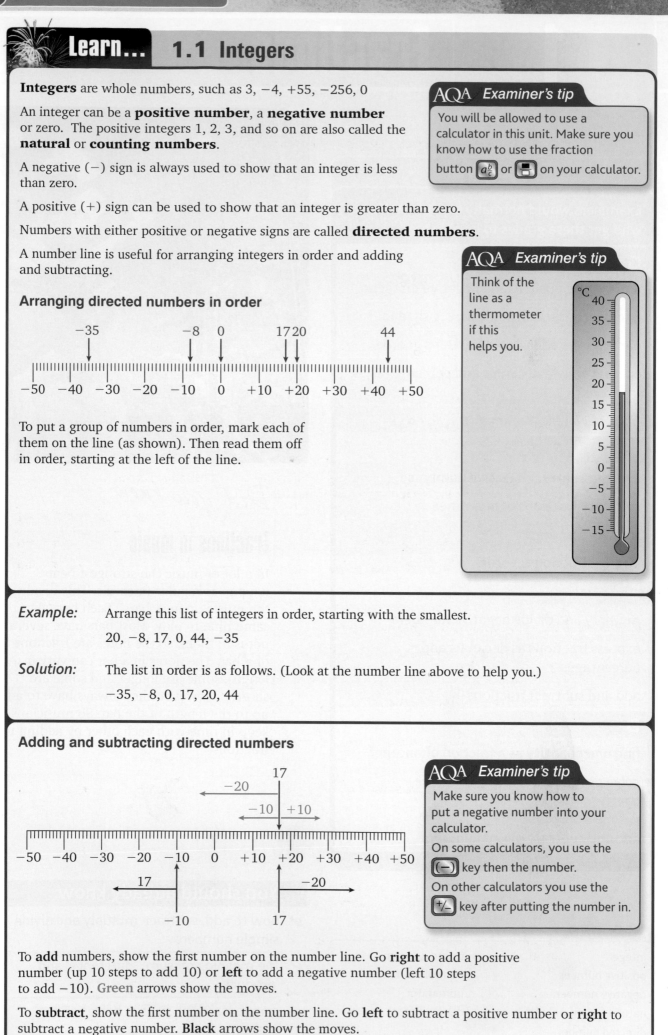

To put a group of numbers in order, mark each of them on the line (as shown). Then read them off in order, starting at the left of the line.

Example: Arrange this list of integers in order, starting with the smallest.

20, −8, 17, 0, 44, −35

Solution: The list in order is as follows. (Look at the number line above to help you.)

−35, −8, 0, 17, 20, 44

Adding and subtracting directed numbers

To **add** numbers, show the first number on the number line. Go **right** to add a positive number (up 10 steps to add 10) or **left** to add a negative number (left 10 steps to add −10). Green arrows show the moves.

To **subtract**, show the first number on the number line. Go **left** to subtract a positive number or **right** to subtract a negative number. **Black** arrows show the moves.

Example: Calculate:

a	$17 + 10$	**c**	$17 + -20$	**e**	$-10 - 17$	**g**	$17 - -20$
b	$17 + -10$	**d**	$17 - 10$	**f**	$17 - -10$		

Solution: See number line above or use your calculator.

a	27	**c**	-3	**e**	-27	**g**	37
b	7	**d**	7	**f**	27		

Practise...   1.1 Integers

G F E D C

1   Arrange each list of integers in order of size, starting with the smallest.

   a $+5$, -12, 0, $+6$, -3, $+10$, -5, -4, $+8$

   b -25, 14, -20, -35, 13, 15, -19, 0, -33

   c 98, -77, 55, -100, 167, -123, 76

   Which set of numbers has the largest difference between the smallest number and the largest number?

2   Work out these additions and subtractions. Look at the sequences of questions and answers to help you to understand the calculations.

   a   **i** $3 + 2$ **ii** $3 + 1$ **iii** $3 + 0$ **iv** $3 + -1$ **v** $3 + -2$ **vi** $3 + -3$ **vii** $3 + -4$

   b   **i** $3 - 2$ **ii** $3 - 1$ **iii** $3 - 0$ **iv** $3 - -1$ **v** $3 - -2$ **vi** $3 - -3$ **vii** $3 - -4$

   c   **i** $3 + -2$ **ii** $3 + -1$ **iii** $3 + 0$ **iv** $3 + +1$ **v** $3 + +2$ **vi** $3 + +3$ **vii** $3 + +4$

   d   **i** $3 - -2$ **ii** $3 - -1$ **iii** $3 - 0$ **iv** $3 - +1$ **v** $3 - +2$ **vi** $3 - +3$ **vii** $3 - +4$

3   **a**   Write down six different pairs of integers that add up to 4

   b   Write down six different pairs of integers that add up to -4

   c   Write down six different pairs of integers that add up to 0

   d   What can you say about a pair of integers that add up to 0?

4   Arrange these numbers in order, starting with the smallest.

   5.2, -2.1, -2.8, 4.5, -0.8, 0.8

   What is the difference between the smallest and the largest of these numbers?

5   Find the value of x in each case.

   a $4 - x = 2$ **b** $4 - x = -2$ **c** $4 - x = 4$ **d** $4 - x = 8$

6   Just before payday, Aaron has an overdraft of £120 in his bank account.
   How much will he have when his salary of £1400 is paid in?

7   Anne has £200 in her bank account. She takes out £350.
   How much is in her account now?

8   Keith owes his friend £1050. He pays £300.

   a   How much does he still owe?

   b   Write this calculation as an addition sum.

9 The table shows the temperatures in different parts of the world.

Which of these statements are correct?

A   The range of temperatures was 40 °C.

B   Rome was 18 °C hotter than the South Pole on this day.

C   Manchester was 10 °C hotter than Montreal.

D   Rome was twice as hot as Tromsø.

E   The difference between the temperature in Manchester and the temperature at the South Pole was 64 °C.

Place	Temperature (°C)
Manchester, UK	24
Montreal, Canada	14
Qaanaaq, Greenland	0
Rome, Italy	22
South Pole	−40
Tromsø, Norway	11

10 Mr Howe sets a 10-question maths test for Year 9. Students got one mark for a correct answer, no marks for a missed question and one mark taken off for a wrong answer.

Fill in the gaps in this table of results.

Name	Correct	Missed	Wrong	Total
Jane	6	1	3	
Apu	3	0	7	
Emma	6	0	4	
Dean	10			10
Calum	4		4	
Kavita	5			2
Amber			5	−1

Jake got a total of −2. Write down three possible ways to get this score.

1.2 Multiplying and dividing positive and negative integers

Learn...

Multiplications of integers can be written as additions.

First, multiply two positive integers.

$+4 \times +3 = +3 + +3 + +3 + +3 = +12$

and

$+4 \times +3 = +4 + +4 + +4 = +12$

These calculations show that two positive numbers multiply together to give a positive number.

Now do a multiplication of a negative integer and a positive integer.

$+4 \times -3 = -3 + -3 + -3 + -3 = -12$

and

$-4 \times +3 = -4 + -4 + -4 = -12$

These calculations show that a positive and a negative number multiply together to give a negative number.

The addition examples above show that changing the sign of one of the numbers in the multiplication changes the sign of the answer.

So, starting with $+4 \times -3 = -12$ and changing $+4$ to -4

the result is $-4 \times -3 = +12$

And starting with $-4 \times +3 = -12$ and changing $+3$ to -3

the result is $-4 \times -3 = +12$

This shows that two negative numbers multiply together to give a positive number.

These multiplication results for positive and negative integers also apply to positive and negative fractions and decimals.

They also apply to division.

So, for example, $+100 \div +20 = +5$

$+100 \div -20 = -5$

$-100 \div +20 = -5$

$-100 \div -20 = +5$

Example: Calculate:

a   **i** $+5 \times +6$ **iii** $+5 \times -6$

ii $-5 \times +6$ **iv** -5×-6

b   **i** $+12 \div +6$ **iii** $+12 \div -6$

ii $-12 \div +6$ **iv** $-12 \div -6$

> **AQA** *Examiner's tip*
> Always recheck your working paying specific attention to the signs.

Solution: **a**   **i** $+30$

ii -30 (because you are multiplying a negative and a positive number)

iii -30 (a positive multiplied by a negative)

iv $+30$ (a negative multiplied by a negative)

b   **i** $+2$ **ii** -2 **iii** -2 **iv** $+2$

Practise...   1.2 **Multiplying and dividing positive and negative integers** 🗨️ G F E D C

1   Which of these calculations give the answer -24?

a $+4 \times +6$ **c** $+4 \times -6$ **e** $+48 \div +2$ **g** $+48 \div -2$

b $-4 \times +6$ **d** -4×-6 **f** $-48 \div +2$ **h** $-48 \div -2$

2   **a**   Write down four different multiplication calculations that give -24.

b   Write down four different division calculations that give -24.

3   Find the missing number in each case.

a $+4 \times \underline{} = -32$ **c** $+5 \times \underline{} = -15$ **e** $-32 \div \underline{} = +4$ **g** $-15 \div \underline{} = +5$

b $\underline{} \times -6 = +36$ **d** $+\frac{1}{2} \times -6 = \underline{}$ **f** $\underline{} \div -6 = -6$ **h** $\underline{} \div -6 = +\frac{1}{2}$

⚠ 4   Work out:

a $-4(5 - 3)$ **c** $\dfrac{15 \times -4}{-2}$ **e** $-\frac{1}{2}(5 - 3)$ **g** $\dfrac{1.5 \times -4}{-2}$

b $-4(3 - 5)$ **d** $\dfrac{12 \times -3}{-2 \times 6}$ **f** $-0.5(2.5 - 0.5)$ **h** $\dfrac{12 \times -3}{-2 \times 0.5}$

❓ 5   How many multiplications of positive and negative integers are there with an answer of -6? Explain how you know you have found them all.

❓ 6   Work out:

a -1×-1 **b** $-1 \times -1 \times -1$ **c** $-1 \times -1 \times -1 \times -1$

What is the result of multiplying five negative ones, six negative ones, seven negative ones, 100 negative ones or 101 negative ones?

Explain how to find the answer when multiplying any number of negative ones.

E

Learn... 1.3 Fractions 🄚

Numbers between integers are expressed using fractions or decimals. They can be positive or negative.

The number lines below show the numbers from 0 to 5 expressed in different ways.

You could imagine these number lines are rulers. Compare them with your own ruler and with each other. Notice what is the same and what is different.

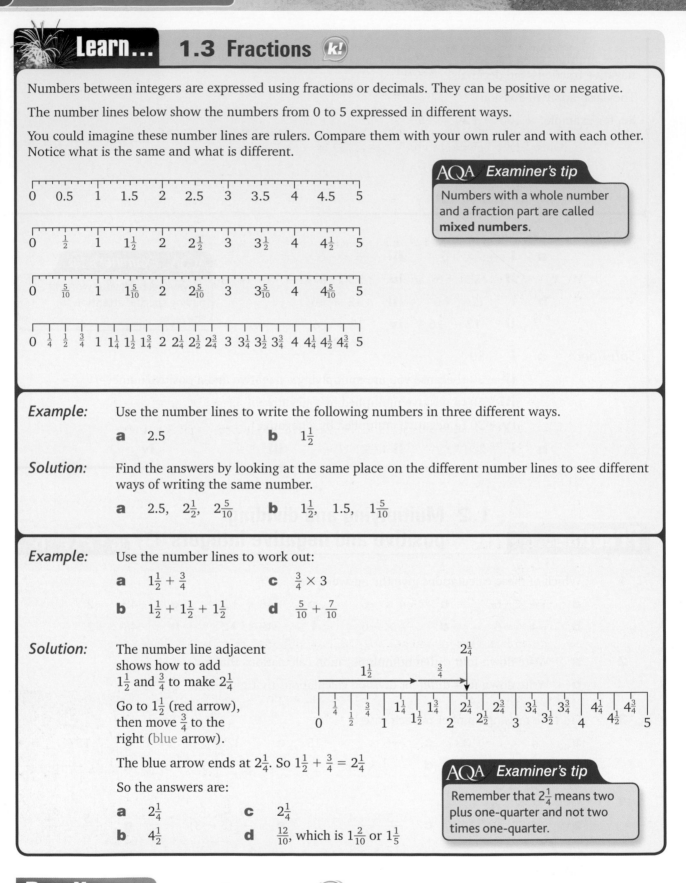

> AQA **Examiner's tip**
>
> Numbers with a whole number and a fraction part are called **mixed numbers**.

Example: Use the number lines to write the following numbers in three different ways.

   a   2.5   **b** $1\frac{1}{2}$

Solution: Find the answers by looking at the same place on the different number lines to see different ways of writing the same number.

   a   2.5, $2\frac{1}{2}$, $2\frac{5}{10}$ **b** $1\frac{1}{2}$, 1.5, $1\frac{5}{10}$

Example: Use the number lines to work out:

   a $1\frac{1}{2} + \frac{3}{4}$ **c** $\frac{3}{4} \times 3$

   b $1\frac{1}{2} + 1\frac{1}{2} + 1\frac{1}{2}$ **d** $\frac{5}{10} + \frac{7}{10}$

Solution: The number line adjacent shows how to add $1\frac{1}{2}$ and $\frac{3}{4}$ to make $2\frac{1}{4}$

Go to $1\frac{1}{2}$ (red arrow), then move $\frac{3}{4}$ to the right (blue arrow).

The blue arrow ends at $2\frac{1}{4}$. So $1\frac{1}{2} + \frac{3}{4} = 2\frac{1}{4}$

So the answers are:

   a $2\frac{1}{4}$ **c** $2\frac{1}{4}$

   b $4\frac{1}{2}$ **d** $\frac{12}{10}$, which is $1\frac{2}{10}$ or $1\frac{1}{5}$

> AQA **Examiner's tip**
>
> Remember that $2\frac{1}{4}$ means two plus one-quarter and not two times one-quarter.

Practise... 1.3 Fractions 🄚   G F E D C

G

1   **a**   Arrange each list of numbers in order of size, starting with the smallest.

   i   4.5, 1.5, 0, 1, 0.5, 3.5, 4

   ii   1.6, 0.8, 3.2, 0.5, 5.0, 4.1

   iii   4.5, $2\frac{1}{2}$, 3.0, $1\frac{5}{10}$, 1.5, $3\frac{1}{2}$, $3\frac{1}{4}$

   b   Which set of numbers has the largest range?

2 A fraction can be expressed as a percentage, for example, $\frac{1}{2} = 50\%$

Copy and complete the following:

$\frac{1}{4} = \underline{\quad}\%$ $\qquad\qquad$ $\frac{3}{4} = \underline{\quad}\%$

3 Work out these additions and subtractions. Look at the sequences of questions and answers to help you to understand the fractions.

a **i** $2\frac{1}{2} + \frac{1}{4}$ $\quad$ **ii** $2\frac{1}{2} + \frac{1}{2}$ $\quad$ **iii** $2\frac{1}{2} + \frac{3}{4}$ $\quad$ **iv** $2\frac{1}{2} + 1$ $\quad$ **v** $2\frac{1}{2} + 1\frac{1}{4}$

b **i** $2\frac{1}{2} + \frac{1}{10}$ $\quad$ **ii** $2\frac{1}{2} + \frac{2}{10}$ $\quad$ **iii** $2\frac{1}{2} + \frac{3}{10}$ $\quad$ **iv** $2\frac{1}{2} + \frac{4}{5}$ $\quad$ **v** $2\frac{1}{2} + \frac{5}{10}$

c **i** $2\frac{1}{2} - \frac{1}{4}$ $\quad$ **ii** $2\frac{1}{2} - \frac{1}{2}$ $\quad$ **iii** $2\frac{1}{2} - \frac{3}{4}$ $\quad$ **iv** $2\frac{1}{2} - 1$ $\quad$ **v** $2\frac{1}{2} - 1\frac{1}{4}$

d Write down the next two calculations in each sequence.

4 Write down three different addition and subtraction calculations that make each of these answers.

a 4.5 $\qquad$ **b** $3\frac{1}{2}$ $\qquad$ **c** $2\frac{1}{4}$ $\qquad$ **d** 0 $\qquad$ **e** $\frac{1}{10}$

5 Work out:

a **i** $3 \times \frac{1}{2}$ $\quad$ **ii** $3 \times 1\frac{1}{2}$ $\quad$ **iii** $3 \times 2\frac{1}{2}$ $\quad$ **iv** $3 \times 3\frac{1}{2}$

b **i** $1 \times \frac{3}{4}$ $\quad$ **ii** $2 \times \frac{3}{4}$ $\quad$ **iii** $3 \times \frac{3}{4}$ $\quad$ **iv** $4 \times \frac{3}{4}$ $\quad$ **v** $5 \times \frac{3}{4}$

c Jenny notices that in these multiplications the answers are smaller than the number being multiplied. Explain why.

6 Sort these fractions out into three sets: less than $\frac{1}{2}$, equal to $\frac{1}{2}$, greater than $\frac{1}{2}$

$\frac{5}{10}, \quad \frac{3}{4}, \quad 0.6, \quad \frac{3}{10}, \quad \frac{1}{4}, \quad \frac{4}{5}, \quad \frac{7}{10}, \quad \frac{2}{4}$

⚠ 7 Complete these sets of fractions.

a $\dfrac{1}{2} = \dfrac{\quad}{2x} = \dfrac{y}{\underline{\quad}} = \dfrac{\quad}{z}$

b $\dfrac{\quad}{\underline{\quad}} = \dfrac{2a}{3a} = \dfrac{2b}{\underline{\quad}} = \dfrac{\quad}{6c} = \dfrac{\quad}{d}$

⚙ 8 The London Eye takes half an hour to travel the full 360° journey. How many degrees does it turn in quarter of an hour?

⚙ 9 At the gym, Nick spends a quarter of an hour on weights, three-quarters of an hour on the running machine and half an hour in the pool.
How much time is this in total?

⚙ 10 The lengths of notes in music are fractions of one another.

Whole note 𝅝 Half a note 𝅗𝅥 Quarter of a note 𝅘𝅥 Eighth of a note 𝅘𝅥𝅮

Add up the notes to find which of these sequences are equivalent to a whole note.
(For example, in **a** there are four quarter notes. This is equivalent to one whole note because $\frac{1}{4} + \frac{1}{4} + \frac{1}{4} + \frac{1}{4} = 1$)

Invent a note sequence of your own equivalent to one whole note.

Learn... 1.4 Equivalent fractions

Equivalent fractions are fractions that are equal in value, such as $\frac{1}{2}$ and $\frac{2}{4}$

In the last section, the number lines showed many other equivalent fractions.

This diagram shows that $\frac{9}{12}$ is equivalent to $\frac{3}{4}$

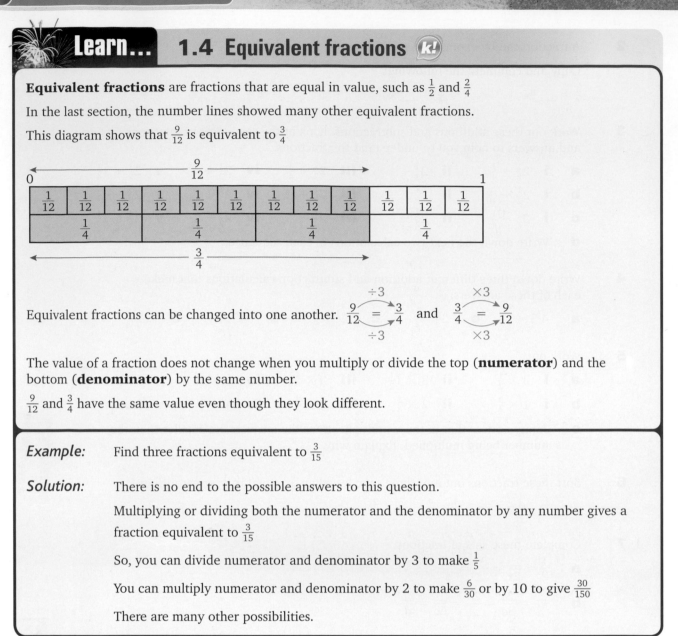

Equivalent fractions can be changed into one another. $\frac{9}{12} \xrightarrow[\div 3]{\div 3} \frac{3}{4}$ and $\frac{3}{4} \xrightarrow[\times 3]{\times 3} \frac{9}{12}$

The value of a fraction does not change when you multiply or divide the top (**numerator**) and the bottom (**denominator**) by the same number.

$\frac{9}{12}$ and $\frac{3}{4}$ have the same value even though they look different.

Example: Find three fractions equivalent to $\frac{3}{15}$

Solution: There is no end to the possible answers to this question.

Multiplying or dividing both the numerator and the denominator by any number gives a fraction equivalent to $\frac{3}{15}$

So, you can divide numerator and denominator by 3 to make $\frac{1}{5}$

You can multiply numerator and denominator by 2 to make $\frac{6}{30}$ or by 10 to give $\frac{30}{150}$

There are many other possibilities.

Practise... 1.4 Equivalent fractions

G F E D C

For Questions 1–3, use your calculator to simplify the fractions. Type in any fraction using the $\boxed{a\frac{b}{c}}$ or $\boxed{\blacksquare}$ key and then press $\boxed{=}$ to find its simplest form.

1 **a** Write down the simplest equivalent fraction for each of these.

  i $\frac{2}{12}$ iii $\frac{4}{12}$ v $\frac{8}{12}$ vii $\frac{10}{12}$

  ii $\frac{3}{12}$ iv $\frac{6}{12}$ vi $\frac{9}{12}$ viii $\frac{12}{12}$

b **i** List the fractions with a denominator of 12 that cannot be made simpler.

  ii Explain why they cannot be made simpler.

2 Find the odd fraction out in this list: $\frac{8}{10}, \frac{6}{8}, \frac{4}{5}, \frac{16}{20}$

Now do the question by changing each of the fractions to decimal form.

G

3 Jack says that $\frac{3}{5} = \frac{6}{8}$

Is he correct? Explain your answer.

4 Write down five fractions that are equivalent to $\frac{2}{3}$

5 Simplify these fractions.

a i $\frac{3}{9}$ ii $\frac{6}{9}$ iii $\frac{9}{9}$

b i $\frac{10}{100}$ iii $\frac{30}{100}$ v $\frac{50}{100}$ vii $\frac{70}{100}$ ix $\frac{90}{100}$

 ii $\frac{20}{100}$ Iv $\frac{40}{100}$ vi $\frac{60}{100}$ viii $\frac{80}{100}$ x $\frac{100}{100}$

c i $\frac{2}{18}$ iii $\frac{4}{18}$ v $\frac{8}{18}$ vii $\frac{10}{18}$ ix $\frac{14}{18}$ xi $\frac{18}{18}$

 ii $\frac{3}{18}$ iv $\frac{6}{18}$ vi $\frac{9}{18}$ viii $\frac{12}{18}$ x $\frac{16}{18}$

d i $\frac{16}{24}$ ii $\frac{25}{30}$ iii $\frac{24}{36}$ iv $\frac{28}{24}$ v $\frac{36}{48}$ vi $\frac{24}{60}$

6 Simplify these fractions.

a $\frac{16}{24}$ c $\frac{24}{36}$ e $\frac{36}{48}$

b $\frac{25}{30}$ d $\frac{28}{42}$ f $\frac{24}{60}$

7 Find **a** two fractions with a denominator of 24 that can be simplified and **b** two fractions with a denominator of 24 that cannot be simplified.

8 Copy and complete these equivalent fraction statements.

a i $\frac{5}{9} = \frac{}{18}$ ii $\frac{8}{9} = \frac{}{18}$ iii $\frac{}{9} = \frac{4}{18}$ iv $\frac{}{9} = \frac{14}{18}$

b i $\frac{1}{6} = \frac{}{24}$ ii $\frac{5}{6} = \frac{}{24}$ iii $\frac{}{6} - \frac{4}{24}$ iv $\frac{}{6} = \frac{12}{24}$

c i $\frac{6}{12} = \frac{}{4} = \frac{}{2}$ ii $\frac{1}{4} = \frac{}{8} = \frac{}{16} = \frac{}{40} = \frac{50}{}$

9 This is a fraction wall diagram.

$\frac{1}{10}$	$\frac{1}{10}$	$\frac{1}{10}$	$\frac{1}{10}$	$\frac{1}{10}$	$\frac{1}{10}$	$\frac{1}{10}$	$\frac{1}{10}$	$\frac{1}{10}$	$\frac{1}{10}$
$\frac{1}{5}$		$\frac{1}{5}$		$\frac{1}{5}$		$\frac{1}{5}$		$\frac{1}{5}$	
$\frac{1}{2}$						$\frac{1}{2}$			

Use this diagram to copy and complete these equivalent fraction statements.

a $\frac{3}{5} = \frac{6}{}$ b $\frac{}{} = \frac{1}{2}$ c $\frac{}{10} = \frac{}{5} = \frac{}{2} = 1$

10 Write down three equivalent fraction statements about:

a   sixths, twelfths and eighteenths

b   tenths, twentieths and hundredths.

F

F

11 Fractions can be marked on a grid like this one. The dot shows $\frac{1}{4}$, because its numerator is 1 and its denominator is 4.

a Make a grid like this, going up to 12 in each direction.

b Mark all the fractions that are equivalent to 1 ($\frac{1}{1}$, $\frac{2}{2}$, $\frac{3}{3}$, etc).
What do you notice?

c Mark two more sets of equivalent fractions on the grid. Compare one set with the other.
What is the same and what is different?

d Where do top-heavy (improper) fractions appear on the grid?

e How can the grid help you to arrange fractions in order?

f How can the grid help you to simplify fractions?

Denominator

F
E

12 This is a fraction wall diagram.

$\frac{1}{16}$	$\frac{1}{16}$	$\frac{1}{16}$	$\frac{1}{16}$	$\frac{1}{16}$	$\frac{1}{16}$	$\frac{1}{16}$	$\frac{1}{16}$	$\frac{1}{16}$	$\frac{1}{16}$	$\frac{1}{16}$	$\frac{1}{16}$	$\frac{1}{16}$	$\frac{1}{16}$	$\frac{1}{16}$	$\frac{1}{16}$
$\frac{1}{8}$		$\frac{1}{8}$		$\frac{1}{8}$		$\frac{1}{8}$		$\frac{1}{8}$		$\frac{1}{8}$		$\frac{1}{8}$		$\frac{1}{8}$	
$\frac{1}{4}$				$\frac{1}{4}$				$\frac{1}{4}$				$\frac{1}{4}$			
$\frac{1}{2}$								$\frac{1}{2}$							
$\frac{1}{1}$															

a Use the fraction wall to write down three equivalent fraction statements.

b **i** Use the fraction wall to write down three fractions that are equivalent to the whole number 1.

ii What can you say about the numerator and the denominator of a fraction that is equivalent to 1?

iii Which fractions in this list are equivalent to 1?

$\frac{100}{100}$ $\quad$ $\frac{2\frac{1}{2}}{2\frac{1}{2}}$ $\quad$ $\frac{200}{100}$ $\quad$ $\frac{x}{x}$ $\quad$ $\frac{2x}{2x}$ $\quad$ $\frac{2x}{x}$ $\quad$ $\frac{x}{2x}$ $\quad$ $\frac{a}{a}$

iv Which fractions in the list above are equivalent to 2?

E

13 A bar of chocolate is split into 24 equal pieces and Sam eats 4 of them.

Joe has another bar of chocolate the same size that is split into 30 equal pieces.

How many pieces of that bar should Joe eat so that he eats the same amount of chocolate as Sam?

14 Mrs Howes marks Year 9's homework. She changes marks out of 20 to marks out of 100 (percentages).

Copy and complete these statements about the marks.

a $\frac{10}{20} = \frac{}{100} = 50\%$

c $\frac{16}{20} = \frac{}{100} = \underline{\quad}\%$

b $\frac{5}{20} = \frac{}{100} = \underline{\quad}\%$

d $\frac{}{20} = \frac{}{100} = 75\%$

Learn... 1.5 Arranging fractions in order (k!)

Equivalent fractions help you to put fractions in order of size.

Change the fractions to equivalent fractions all with the same denominator, then compare the size of the fractions by looking at the numerators.

AQA Examiner's tip

Another method of arranging fractions in order is to change each fraction to a decimal. You do this by dividing the numerator by the denominator (find out why this works). Then put the decimals in order.

Example: (k!) Arrange the following fractions in order of size, smallest first.

$$\frac{2}{3} \quad \frac{1}{4} \quad \frac{5}{6} \quad \frac{1}{12} \quad \frac{1}{2}$$

Solution: In order to put fractions in order of size, first change them all to the same denominator.

$$\frac{2}{3} \quad \frac{1}{4} \quad \frac{5}{6} \quad \frac{1}{12} \quad \frac{1}{2}$$

All the denominators go into 12 exactly,
so 12 is a good number for the denominator.

Change the fractions to twelfths: $\frac{2}{3} \xrightarrow{\times 4} \frac{8}{12}$ and so on.

So the list $\quad \frac{2}{3} \quad \frac{1}{4} \quad \frac{5}{6} \quad \frac{1}{12} \quad \frac{1}{2}$ becomes $\quad \frac{8}{12} \quad \frac{3}{12} \quad \frac{10}{12} \quad \frac{1}{12} \quad \frac{6}{12}$

In order of size this is $\quad \frac{1}{12} \quad \frac{3}{12} \quad \frac{6}{12} \quad \frac{8}{12} \quad \frac{10}{12}$ or $\quad \frac{1}{12} \quad \frac{1}{4} \quad \frac{1}{2} \quad \frac{2}{3} \quad \frac{5}{6}$

Practise... 1.5 Arranging fractions in order (k!)   F

All these questions can be done without a calculator and you should make sure that you are able to do without. Also make sure that you can use your calculator to speed up and check your work, using your $\boxed{a\frac{b}{c}}$ or $\boxed{\Box}$ key if you have one.

1

a Change these fractions to twelfths and arrange them in order from smallest to largest.

$$\frac{3}{4} \quad \frac{1}{3} \quad \frac{5}{12} \quad \frac{1}{6} \quad \frac{1}{2}$$

b Change these fractions to fifteenths and arrange them in order from smallest to largest.

$$\frac{3}{5} \quad \frac{2}{3} \quad \frac{7}{15} \quad \frac{4}{15}$$

c Change these fractions to hundredths and arrange them in order from smallest to largest.

$$\frac{3}{4} \quad \frac{1}{5} \quad \frac{7}{20} \quad \frac{3}{10} \quad \frac{1}{2} \quad \frac{57}{100} \quad \frac{8}{25} \quad \frac{13}{50}$$

Fractions with a denominator of 100 are percentages, for example $\frac{70}{100}$ is 70%

2 Arrange these fractions in order of size: $\frac{2}{3} \quad \frac{2}{5} \quad \frac{1}{2} \quad \frac{7}{10}$

F

3 **a** What is a good denominator for ordering each of the following?

    i Thirds, quarters and sixths

    ii Fifths, twentieths and fiftieths

b Explain why it is not easy to change fifths to twelfths.

4 **a** Abby says 'Five-eighths is smaller than five-twelfths.' Is she correct?

b Ali says 'Four-fifths is smaller than five-sixths.' Is he correct?

5 Find a fraction that is:

a between one-half and three-quarters

b between nine-tenths and one.

Learn... 1.6 Fractions of quantities

To work out three-quarters of a number, first find one-quarter of it, then multiply that by three to find three-quarters.

Example: There are 54 teachers in a school. Two-thirds of the teachers are female.

How many female teachers are there in the school?

Solution: To find the number of female teachers you need to find $\frac{2}{3}$ of 54.

To work out two-thirds of 54, first work out one-third of 54, then multiply the answer by two to find two-thirds.

$\frac{1}{3}$ of 54 = 54 ÷ 3 = 18

So

$\frac{2}{3}$ of 54 = 2 × 18 = 36

So there are 36 female teachers in the school.

It doesn't matter whether you divide by three and then multiply by two or multiply by two and then divide by three. The result is the same.

Practise... 1.6 Fractions of quantites (k!)

1   Work out two-thirds of these values.

     a   15   **c**   £1800   **e**   £1900 (give your answer to the nearest penny).

     b   120   **d**   £5391

2   **a**   Two-thirds of a number is 10. What is the number?

     b   Two-thirds of a number is 20. What is the number?

3   Work out three-fifths of these values.

     a   £150   **b**   £1900   **c**   £19.75   **d**   £154 800   **e**   £1 million.

4   Which of these calculations will work out $\frac{3}{5}$ of 44?
Write down all of the calculations that apply.

     a $44 \div 5 \times 3$ **c** $44 \times 5 \div 3$ **e** $44 \div 100 \times 60$

     b $44 \div 3 \times 5$ **d** $44 \times 3 \div 5$ **f** $44 \times 10 \div 6$

5   Work out $\frac{3}{4}$ of 20.

Now find $\frac{4}{3}$ of the answer.
What do you notice?
Can you explain what has happened?
Try this with another number.

6   Pastry is two-thirds flour and one-third fat.
How much flour is there in 180 g of pastry?

How much pastry can you make if you have
50 g of flour?

7   A type of bronze used to make coins is made up of copper, tin and zinc.

$\frac{95}{100}$ of the bronze is copper, $\frac{4}{100}$ is tin and the rest is zinc.

How much zinc is there in 2 kg of bronze?

Learn... 1.7 One quantity as a fraction of another

Mathematics is often used to make comparisons. For example, fractions (or percentages) can be used to compare the proportion of people who benefit from one medical treatment rather than another. To do this, you need to be able to work out one quantity as a fraction (or percentage) of another. To work out 35 as a fraction of 50, write 35 out of 50 as a fraction, $\frac{35}{50}$, then simplify to $\frac{7}{10}$. So 35 is seven-tenths of 50.

(To express 35 as a percentage of 50, change $\frac{7}{10}$ to an equivalent fraction with a denominator of 100.
So 35 is $\frac{70}{100}$, or 70%, of 50.)

Example: 16 students out of 28 passed a maths test.
What fraction of the students passed?

Solution: The fraction is $\frac{16}{28}$. This simplifies to $\frac{4}{7}$

This result could also be expressed as a decimal or a percentage. In everyday life percentages are usually used.

Practise... 1.7 One quantity as a fraction of another

1 a All 28 students in a class took a test. Work out the fraction of them that passed if the number passing was as follows.

  i 14   ii 12   iii 13   iv 18   v 20

  b If the fraction passing the test was $\frac{3}{4}$, how many students passed?

  c Explain why you will never get an improper (top-heavy) fraction in a question like this.

2 In a dance class there are 25 women and 15 men.

  a What is the fraction of men in the class?

  b What is the fraction of women in the class?

3 One day Kevin sold 10 pounds of chocolates. 75% of them were milk chocolates, 10% were white chocolates and the rest were plain chocolates.

  What weight of plain chocolates did he sell?

4 Here is a list of the test marks of a class of 30 students, arranged in order.

  a What fraction of the students got under 40 marks?

  b What fraction of the students got a mark in the sixties?

  c The pass mark was 50 marks. What fraction of the students passed the test?

  d What should the pass mark be for two-thirds of the students to pass the test?

  e What mark separates the top tenth of the class from the rest?

```
22  25
30  33  37
42  43  46  46
53  54  55  55  56
61  61  63  64  64  67  68  68  69
73  75  78  79
81  87
95
```

5

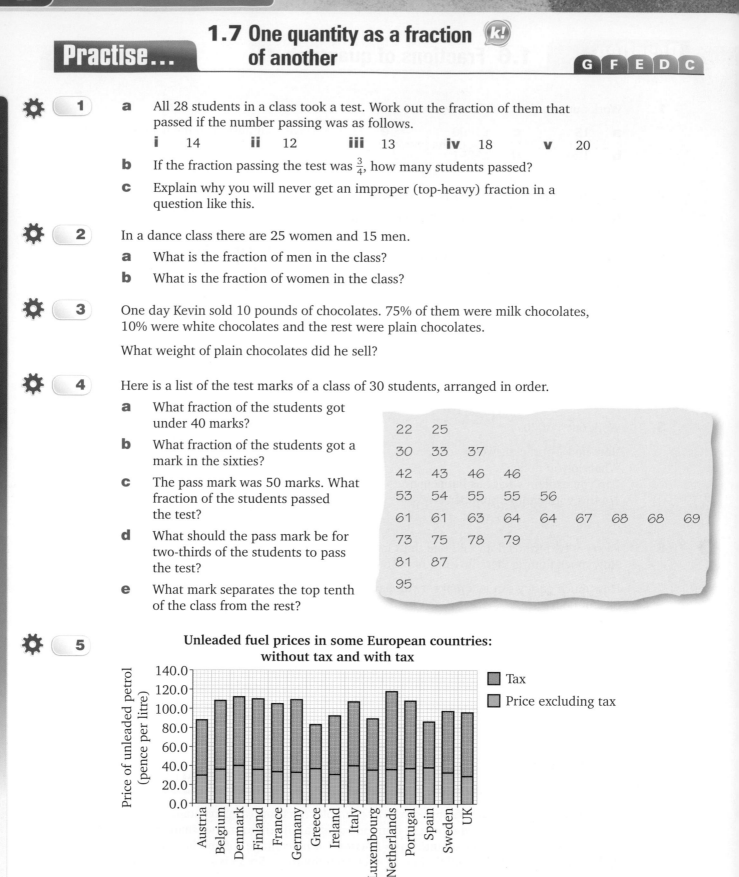

Unleaded fuel prices in some European countries: without tax and with tax

(Data obtained from: http://stats.berr.gov.uk. Premium unleaded petrol prices in the EU, April 2009)

The graph shows how the total price paid for unleaded petrol is made up.

  a Estimate the fraction of the total price paid in tax in the UK.

  b Which country pays the highest fraction in tax?

  c Which country pays the lowest?

  d Would it affect your answers if the prices were in euros instead of in pence? Explain your answer.

1 Assess

1 Fill in the spaces with one of the following phrases: 'is greater than' or 'is less than'.

$$4 \ldots\ldots\ldots 10 \qquad\qquad -4 \ldots\ldots\ldots -10$$

$$10 \ldots\ldots\ldots 4 \qquad\qquad -10 \ldots\ldots\ldots -4$$

2 a What fraction of the shape is shaded?

b What fraction is not shaded?

3 Match each percentage with an equivalent fraction.

75%   20%   45%   90%   15%

$\frac{1}{5}$ $\frac{3}{20}$ $\frac{9}{20}$ $\frac{3}{4}$ $\frac{9}{10}$

4 What are the missing numbers that make these fractions equivalent?

$$\frac{3}{7} = \frac{\quad}{21} = \frac{24}{\quad}$$

5 Continue these sequences of numbers.

a 5, 3, 1, −1, ___ , ___ , ___

(Each number is two less than the one before.)

b −3, −1, −4, ___ , ___ , ___

(Each number is the sum of the two previous numbers.)

6 Work out:

a $\frac{1}{5}$ of £50   **b** $\frac{5}{8}$ of £50   **c** $\frac{3}{8}$ of 0.52

7 a Change these fractions to equivalent fractions with denominator sixteen and then put them in order of size, starting with the smallest.

$\frac{3}{8}$ $\frac{1}{4}$ $\frac{7}{8}$ $\frac{9}{48}$

b Arrange these fractions in order of size, smallest first.

$\frac{2}{3}$ $\frac{5}{8}$ $\frac{7}{12}$ $\frac{11}{24}$

c Which is smaller, $\frac{2}{5}$ or $\frac{3}{8}$?

8 Paula is running a 10 000 m race.

How far has she run when she has covered $\frac{5}{8}$ of it?

9 This sequence of fractions goes down in equal steps. $1\frac{7}{8}$ $1\frac{5}{8}$ $1\frac{3}{8}$ ...

Write down the next three terms of the sequence.

10 Mrs Snow travels 480 miles to Scotland.

360 miles are on motorways.

What fraction of the journey is on motorways?

D

11 A train arrived at St Pancras station 30 minutes late.
What fraction is this of the timetabled journey time of $2\frac{1}{2}$ hours?

12 240 students take an exam. 100 students answered question 3 correctly.
What fraction get the question wrong?

13 A car costs £3500. The price is reduced by one-fifth. The deposit is one-quarter of the reduced price.
How much is the deposit?

14 The table shows the mean temperature in degrees Celsius each month in Anchorage, Alaska, USA.

Jan	Feb	Mar	Apr	May	Jun	Jul	Aug	Sep	Oct	Nov	Dec
−10	−7	−4	2	8	12	15	14	9	1	−6	−9

a Which is the coldest month in Anchorage?

b For what fraction of the year is the mean temperature above zero?

c What is the difference in mean temperature between the coldest month and the hottest month?

15 Here are some computer game scores.

a Who has the highest score?

b Who has the lowest score?

c Which two people's scores add up to zero?

d Which score is the most common?

e Whose score is the middle one?

Susan	2500
Roy	−100
Dave	−1500
Carl	2000
Kate	2500
Paul	3250
Naz	−250
Hafsa	0
Mike	250

16 In a sale the price of a coat, originally £84, is reduced by $\frac{1}{3}$
What is the sale price of the coat?

AQA Examination-style questions

1 There are 175 pupils in Year 10 at a school.

    a $\frac{2}{5}$ of these pupils own a dog.

       How many pupils in Year 10 own a dog? *(2 marks)*

    b Alice says that exactly half of the Year 10 pupils are boys.

       Explain why Alice must be wrong. *(1 mark)*

    c The number of pupils in Year 10 is one-eighth of the total number of pupils in the school.

       Work out the total number of pupils in the school. *(2 marks)*

AQA 2008

Decimals

Objectives

Examiners would normally expect students who get these grades to be able to:

G

round to the nearest integer

F

write down the place value of a decimal digit such as the value of 3 in 0.63

order decimals such as 0.46 and 0.5

round numbers to given powers of 10 and to a given number of decimal places

E

round a number to one significant figure

add, subtract and multiply decimals

estimate answers to calculations involving decimals

convert simple fractions to decimals and decimals to fractions

D

multiply decimals.

Did you know?

In many sports, gold medals are won by fractions of a second.

Years ago the winner in a swimming competition was the first person to be seen to touch the wall by the referee or judge. Today, electronic sensors give the finish time to the nearest one hundredth of a second so that the winner can be found even in the closest of races.

In the Beijing Olympic Games of 2008, Michael Phelps won eight gold medals. In the 100 metre Butterfly Final Phelps' time was 50.58 seconds. He beat the second place swimmer by 0.01 seconds.

Key terms

decimal
integer
digit
decimal place
round
significant figures
numerator
denominator

You should already know:

✔ how to arrange whole numbers in order of size

✔ how to add, subtract, multiply and divide whole numbers.

Learn... 2.1 Place value

The **decimal** point separates the whole number or **integer** part from the fraction part.

For example, the number 23.67 can be written in a place value table like this.

Thousands	Hundreds	Tens	Units	.	Tenths	Hundredths	Thousandths
		2	3	.	6	7	

The value of the **digit** 2 is 20. The digit 2 has the highest value so is the most important part of the number. It is called the most **significant figure**.

The value of the digit 3 is 3

The value of the digit 6 is 0.6

The value of the digit 7 is 0.07

Example: Write these numbers in order of size starting with the highest.

2.6   1.48   2.09   1.375

Solution: The numbers should be put into a place value table.

Thousands	Hundreds	Tens	Units	.	Tenths	Hundredths	Thousandths
			2	.	6		
			1	.	4	8	
			2	.	0	9	
			1	.	3	7	5

Compare the most significant values first. In this case this is the units.

There are two numbers starting with 2 so compare the tenths for these two numbers.

2.6 is higher than 2.09 as 6 tenths is higher than 0 tenths.

Compare the numbers starting with a 1 in the same way.

1.48 is higher than 1.375 as 4 tenths is higher than 3 tenths.

So this gives the order:

2.6   2.09   1.48   1.375

> **AQA Examiner's tip**
>
> Make sure you read carefully which order you are asked for. In this case you were asked to start with the highest.

Practise... 2.1 Place value   𝑘!   **G** **F**

1   Write these numbers in a place value table.

17.65   231.4   5.961   0.35   54.702

2   Put each list of numbers in order of size, starting with the highest.

   a   3.4   3.16   3.27   3.19   3.08

   b   24.2   27.68   25.34   24.02   25.75

   c   0.426   0.57   0.623   0.64   0.421

3   Put each list of numbers in order of size, starting with the lowest.

   a   1.4   1.37   1.138   1.09   1.2

   b   15.46   16.54   15.49   17.3   15.0

   c   0.25   0.52   0.325   0.514   0.239

4   Write down the value of the digit 7 in each of these numbers.

   a   2.7   **c**   1.237   **e**   2.47   **g**   723.46

   b   7.34   **d**   2.714   **f**   0.176   **h**   7432.1

Learn...   2.2 Rounding ⓚ

It is often sensible to **round** figures to give an approximate answer.

For example, using a calculator, an area is worked out to be 18.27146 square metres.

This could be rounded to 18 square metres to make the numbers more manageable.

Numbers can be rounded to the nearest integer, nearest 10, nearest 100, etc.

Numbers can also be rounded to decimals, for example 1 **decimal place**, depending on what the information is needed for.

Sometimes a number is exactly halfway between two others.

In this case it is always rounded up to the higher number.

So 17.5 would round up to 18.

Example: Round 17.8 to:

     a   the nearest integer   **b**   the nearest ten.

Solution: **a**

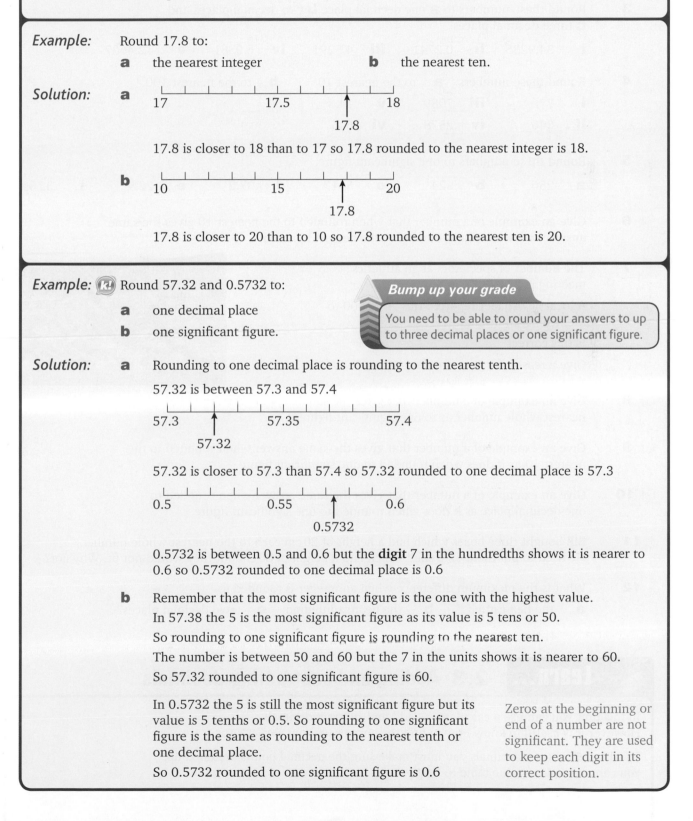

17.8 is closer to 18 than to 17 so 17.8 rounded to the nearest integer is 18.

     b

17.8 is closer to 20 than to 10 so 17.8 rounded to the nearest ten is 20.

Example: ⓚ Round 57.32 and 0.5732 to:

     a   one decimal place

     b   one significant figure.

> **Bump up your grade**
>
> You need to be able to round your answers to up to three decimal places or one significant figure.

Solution: **a**   Rounding to one decimal place is rounding to the nearest tenth.

57.32 is between 57.3 and 57.4

57.32 is closer to 57.3 than 57.4 so 57.32 rounded to one decimal place is 57.3

0.5732 is between 0.5 and 0.6 but the **digit** 7 in the hundredths shows it is nearer to 0.6 so 0.5732 rounded to one decimal place is 0.6

     b   Remember that the most significant figure is the one with the highest value.

In 57.38 the 5 is the most significant figure as its value is 5 tens or 50.

So rounding to one significant figure is rounding to the nearest ten.

The number is between 50 and 60 but the 7 in the units shows it is nearer to 60.

So 57.32 rounded to one significant figure is 60.

In 0.5732 the 5 is still the most significant figure but its value is 5 tenths or 0.5. So rounding to one significant figure is the same as rounding to the nearest tenth or one decimal place.

So 0.5732 rounded to one significant figure is 0.6

Zeros at the beginning or end of a number are not significant. They are used to keep each digit in its correct position.

Practise... 2.2 Rounding

G F E D C

1 Round these to the nearest whole number.
(Use a number line to help you.)

a 4.2   **b** 7.8   **c** 34.6   **d** 0.7   **e** 0.3   **f** 76.5

2 **a** Julian says that 537 rounded to the nearest 10 is 54.
What has he done wrong?

     b Ravi says that 4.3 rounded to the nearest whole number is 5.
Is he correct?
Give a reason for your answer.

3 Round these numbers to **a** one decimal place **b** two decimal places and
c three decimal places.

i 54.9235   **ii** 0.2741   **iii** 4.5291   **iv** 6.0381   **v** 12.4687

4 Round these numbers: **a** to the nearest 10   **b** to the nearest 100.

i 776   **iii** 7089   **v** 14.3
ii 346   **iv** 2578   **vi** 645

5 Round these numbers to one significant figure.

a 256   **b** 324   **c** 5617   **d** 37.2   **e** 22.9   **f** 33 624

6 Give an example of a number that when rounded to the nearest 10 gives the same
answer as it does when rounded to the nearest hundred.

7 The number of spectators at an athletics
meeting is 23 278.

A local newspaper reported this as 24 000 to
the nearest thousand.

Is this correct?

Give a reason for your answer.

8 Give an example of a number that gives the same answer when rounded to the
nearest whole number as to one significant figure.

9 Give an example of a number that gives the same answer when rounded to the
nearest 10 as it does when rounded to one significant figure.

10 Give an example of a number that gives the same answer when rounded to
one decimal place as it does when rounded to one significant figure.

11 Bill bought three boxes which had a height of 20 cm each to the nearest whole number.
He tried to put them on a shelf which had a height of 60 cm but they would not fit. Why not?

12 What is the maximum difference when an integer is rounded to:

a the nearest ten   **b** the nearest hundred   **c** two decimal places?

Learn... 2.3 Adding and subtracting decimals

In this unit you can use a calculator to add and subtract decimals.
However it is useful to know how to find the answer without a calculator.

To add and subtract decimals you must make sure the decimal points are lined up.
You can use a place value table to help you.

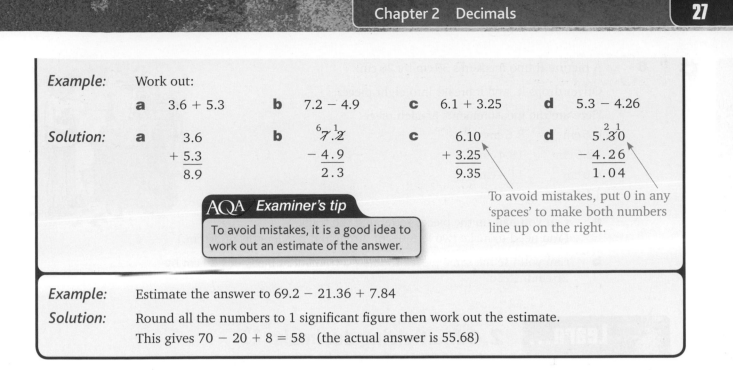

Example: Work out:

  a 3.6 + 5.3   **b** 7.2 − 4.9   **c** 6.1 + 3.25   **d** 5.3 − 4.26

Solution:

a
```
   3.6
 + 5.3
 -----
   8.9
```

b
```
  ⁶7.¹2̸
 − 4.9
 -----
   2.3
```

c
```
   6.10
 + 3.25
 -----
   9.35
```

d
```
   5.²3̸¹0
 − 4.26
 -----
   1.04
```

To avoid mistakes, put 0 in any 'spaces' to make both numbers line up on the right.

AQA **Examiner's tip**

To avoid mistakes, it is a good idea to work out an estimate of the answer.

Example: Estimate the answer to 69.2 − 21.36 + 7.84

Solution: Round all the numbers to 1 significant figure then work out the estimate.
This gives 70 − 20 + 8 = 58   (the actual answer is 55.68)

Practise... 2.3 Adding and subtracting decimals 🎵 G F E D C

1 Work these out without a calculator.

  a 12.2 + 3.9   **c** 8.23 + 7.1   **e** 24.09 + 15.6

  b 1.4 + 5.31   **d** 4.92 − 3.68   **f** 3.92 − 2.48 + 5.63

Check your answers with a calculator.

2 Yusef says that 3.2 + 1.34 = 4.36

Isaac says 3.2 + 1.34 = 4.54

Who is correct?

Give a reason for your answer.

3 Fill in the missing digits (shown as ☺) in these calculations.

  a 2.4 + 1.3 = ☺.7   **c** ☺.2 + 4.1 = 7.3   **e** ☺.7 − 2.8 = 2.☺

  b 3.☺ + 2.4 = 5.8   **d** 5.4 − 1.2 = ☺.2   **f** 9.☺ − 4.2 = ☺.5

4 Andy says that 7.4 − 5.32 = 2.08

Tom says that 7.4 − 5.32 = 2.12

Who made the mistake?

Explain the mistake he made.

5 Estimate the answers to these calculations by rounding to one significant figure.

Use a calculator to check that your estimated answers are close to the exact answers.

  a 2.9 + 3.2   **f** 69.46 − 22.7

  b 7.9 + 2.2   **g** 9.28 − 3.16

  c 67.8 + 22.1   **h** 17.8 − 8.76

  d 20.7 + 38.2   **i** 4.78 + 9.32 − 6.1

  e 102.3 + 97.8   **j** 87.4 − 31.6 + 42.9

E

6 A picture frame measures 30 cm by 20 cm.

Oliver drops it, and it breaks into eight pieces.

Here are the measurements of each piece.

4.6 cm	8.6 cm
12.6 cm	15.4 cm
8.6 cm	11.4 cm
17.4 cm	21.4 cm

a Can you pair up the pieces to rebuild the frame?
(You need to make two lengths of 20 cm and two lengths of 30 cm.)

b Can you use the same pieces to make a frame that measures 24 cm by 26 cm instead?

Learn... 2.4 Multiplying decimals 🔵

In this unit you can use a calculator to multiply decimals.

However it is useful to know how to find the answer without a calculator.

To avoid mistakes, it is a good idea to work out an estimate to the answer.

For example, estimate the answer to 2.83×5.14

Round each number to one significant figure then multiply.

The estimate is $3 \times 5 = 15$

Using a calculator, the exact answer is 14.5462

> **AQA** *Examiner's tip*
>
> Always do a quick estimate of answers in an exam to ensure you have not made errors when you put values into the calculator.

Example: 🔵 Multiply 42×0.3

Solution: First remove the decimal points which gives $42 \times 3 = 126$

Now count up the decimal places in the question.

There is one decimal place in the question 42×0.3

You need one decimal place in the answer, so the answer is 12.6

Practise... 2.4 Multiplying decimals 🔵

1 Calculate:

a	2.1×22	**c**	8.7×2.5	**e**	3.2×2.3	**g**	19.4×3.1
b	1.7×2.2	**d**	3.5×2.3	**f**	73.1×1.9	**h**	8.6×3.7

2 Check your answers to Question 1 are sensible by estimating the answers.

3 For each question, decide which is the best estimate.

		Estimate A	Estimate B	Estimate C
a	3.24×7.9	2.4	21	24
b	2.89×9.4	2.7	18	27
c	1.2×29.4	3	30	300
d	48.5×9.8	5	50	500
e	22.4×6.1	12	120	180
f	16.6×9.9	160	170	1700

D

4 Work out:

    a 0.2×0.2 **c** 0.3×0.5 **e** 0.04×0.1 **g** $0.2 \times 0.1 \times 0.4$

    b 1.3×0.2 **d** 0.12×0.3 **f** 2.1×0.3

5 Toby says $0.4 \times 0.2 = 0.8$

Austin says it isn't, because $4 \times 0.2 = 0.8$

Austin says $0.4 \times 0.2 = 0.08$

Toby says it isn't because that's less than you started with.

Who is right, Toby or Austin?

Give a reason for your answer.

6 Estimate, by rounding each number to one significant figure:

    a $\dfrac{305 \times 4.96}{9.92}$ **b** $\dfrac{2 \times 527.9}{12.3 + 7.8}$

7 A glass contains 0.3 litre of orange juice.

Zoe needs to fill 24 glasses with orange juice.

Work out the total number of litres of orange juice she needs.

8 Rachel is making curtains.

She can choose from two fabrics of different widths.

Fabric A costs £5.20 per metre.   Fabric B is wider. It costs £6.80 per metre.

She will need 9.5 metres of fabric A.   She will need 7.2 metres of fabric B.

Work out the cost of the cheaper curtains.

Learn...   2.5 Fractions and decimals

To change a fraction to a decimal just divide the **numerator** (top number) by the **denominator** (bottom number) on your calculator.

Numerator $\longrightarrow \dfrac{2}{3} \longleftarrow$ Denominator

$\dfrac{3}{8}$ means $3 \div 8$ so $\dfrac{3}{8}$ written as a decimal is 0.375

To change a decimal to a fraction, put the decimal into a place value table.

Example: Write 0.17 as a fraction.

Solution:

Units	.	tenths	hundredths
0	.	1	7

The least significant figure is hundredths so this is the denominator of the fraction.

$0.17 = \dfrac{17}{100}$

Example: Write 0.825 as a fraction.

Solution:

Units	.	tenths	hundredths	thousandths
0	.	8	2	5

The least significant figure is thousandths so this is the denominator of the fraction.

$0.825 = \dfrac{825}{1000}$

This can be cancelled down to a simpler form using your calculator.

Use the $\boxed{a\frac{b}{c}}$ or $\boxed{\blacksquare}$ button to input $\dfrac{825}{1000}$ then press the $\boxed{=}$ button. The calculator will give the simplest form of this fraction which is $\dfrac{33}{40}$

AQA *Examiner's tip*

Check your answer by working backwards.

$33 \div 40 = 0.825$

E

D

Practise... 2.5 Fractions and decimals *k!*

1 Change these fractions to decimals.

a $\frac{4}{5}$ c $\frac{1}{8}$ e $\frac{2}{5}$ g $\frac{3}{25}$

b $\frac{9}{10}$ d $\frac{11}{20}$ f $\frac{1}{4}$ h $\frac{3}{10}$

2 Which of these fractions is closest to 0.67?

a $\frac{3}{4}$ b $\frac{5}{8}$ c $\frac{3}{5}$

3 Write these decimals as fractions.

a 0.23   c 0.3   e 0.2   g 0.35

b 0.09   d 0.31   f 0.77   h 0.127

4 At a school fête, some children decided to raise money with a 'Guess the weight of the cake' competition.

Hannah guessed 2.17 kilograms and Jack guessed $2\frac{3}{5}$ kilograms.

The weight of the cake was 2.45 kilograms.

Whose guess was closest to the real weight?

Show your working.

5 Find two fractions which fit all these rules.

The fractions must have different denominators
Each denominator must be less than 10
The fraction must be greater than 0.4
The fraction must be less than 0.5

2 Assess

G

1 Round each number to the nearest integer.

a 23.4   b 8.6   c 3.275   d 4.812   e 17.549

F

2 Put each list of numbers in order of size, starting with the smallest.

a 5.3   5.07   5.16   5.36   5.069

b 23.567   23.59   23.531   23.099   23.8

c 0.37   0.73   0.337   0.373   0.377

3 Write down the value of the digit 3 in each of these numbers.

a 4.03   c 5.237   e 6.783   g 723.46

b 7.34   d 36.7   f 0.36   h 8342.1

4 17 624 people watch a football match.

Write this number to the nearest:

a 1000   b 10   c 10 000   d 100

5   **a**   Trevor and Paul both like jogging.
One day Trevor jogs 7.25 kilometres.
Paul jogs 2.46 kilometres further than Trevor.

How far does Paul jog?

b   The Olympic triathlon is a race which involves swimming, cycling and running.
The total distance for the race is 31.93 miles.
Competitors swim a distance of 0.93 mile, then cycle a distance of 24.8 miles.
They run the final part of the race.

How far do they run?

6   Jon says that he and Carl are the same weight, to one significant figure.
Jon weighs 76 kilograms.
Carl weighs 82 kilograms.

Is Jon correct?
Explain your answer.

7   Estimate the value of 18.96×4.96

Is your answer an over-estimate or an under-estimate?

8   One kilogram of strawberries costs £1.96

How much do three kilograms of strawberries cost?

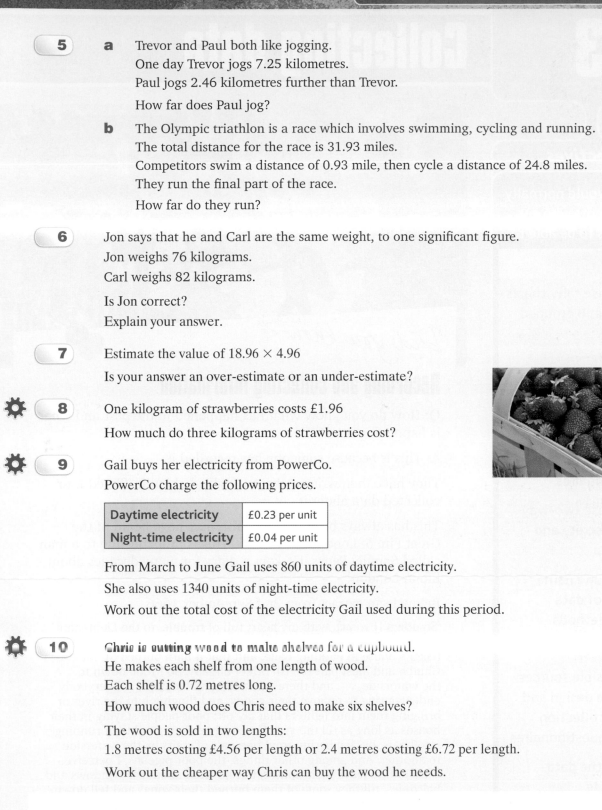

9   Gail buys her electricity from PowerCo.
PowerCo charge the following prices.

Daytime electricity	£0.23 per unit
Night-time electricity	£0.04 per unit

From March to June Gail uses 860 units of daytime electricity.

She also uses 1340 units of night-time electricity.

Work out the total cost of the electricity Gail used during this period.

10   Chris is cutting wood to make shelves for a cupboard.
He makes each shelf from one length of wood.
Each shelf is 0.72 metres long.

How much wood does Chris need to make six shelves?

The wood is sold in two lengths:
1.8 metres costing £4.56 per length or 2.4 metres costing £6.72 per length.

Work out the cheaper way Chris can buy the wood he needs.

AQA Examination-style questions

1   The table shows the cost of photo frames on a website.

Photo frames £5.25 each	Postage and packing	
	Orders under £100	£10.50
	Orders £100 and over	Free

Nikki spent a total of £110.25 on an order with this website.
How many photo frames could Nikki have bought?
Give the **two** possible answers.

(3 marks)

AQA 2009

Collecting data

Objectives

Examiners would normally expect students who get these grades to be able to:

G

design and use tally charts for discrete and grouped data

D

understand and name different types of data

design and use data collection sheets, surveys and questionnaires

design and use two-way tables for discrete and grouped data

understand and name other types of data collection methods

C

identify possible sources of bias in the design and use of data collection sheets and questionnaires

understand the data-handling cycle

understand that increasing sample size generally leads to better estimates.

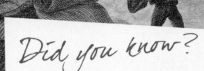

Did you know?

Recording and collecting information

Q: How do you know what has happened in the past and what is happening now?

A: This is because someone has recorded it.

They have then written about it, talked about it, filmed it or collected data about it.

This has always been the case. You may have heard of the Great Fire of London from 1666. This is probably due to a man called Samuel Pepys. He kept a diary for many decades about life in London.

Below is an extract from 2nd September 1666.

'So down [I went], with my heart full of trouble, to the Lieutenant of the Tower, who tells me that it began this morning in the King's baker's house in Pudding Lane, and that it hath burned St. Magnus's Church and most part of Fish Street already. So I rode down to the waterside, . . . and there saw a lamentable fire. . . . Everybody endeavouring to remove their goods, and flinging into the river or bringing them into lighters that lay off; poor people staying in their houses as long as till the very fire touched them, and then running into boats, or clambering from one pair of stairs by the waterside to another. And among other things, the poor pigeons, I perceive, were loth to leave their houses, but hovered about the windows and balconies, till they some of them burned their wings and fell down.'

In statistics you need to think about how data can be collected, recorded and sorted.

You should already know:

✓ how to count in fives for tally charts.

Key terms

hypothesis	population	observation
raw data	sample	controlled experiment
primary data	sample size	data logging
secondary data	questionnaire	tally chart
qualitative data	survey	frequency table
quantitative data	open questions	data collection sheet
discrete data	closed questions	observation sheet
continuous data	pilot survey	two-way table

Learn... 3.1 Types of data

The data-handling cycle is the framework for work in statistics. It has four stages.

The data-handling cycle

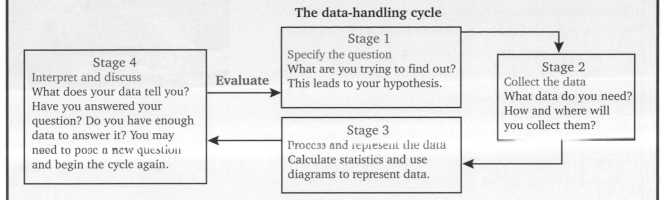

Stage 4	Stage 1	Stage 2
Interpret and discuss What does your data tell you? Have you answered your question? Do you have enough data to answer it? You may need to pose a new question and begin the cycle again.	**Evaluate** → Specify the question What are you trying to find out? This leads to your hypothesis.	Collect the data What data do you need? How and where will you collect them?
	Stage 3 Process and represent the data Calculate statistics and use diagrams to represent data.	

In any statistical project it is usual to go through the data-handling cycle at least once.

The first stage is to decide on what you are trying to find out. This leads to the **hypothesis**, a statement that you want to investigate.

The second stage is to think about what data you need and how to collect it.

The third stage is to make calculations and summarise the collected data using tables and diagrams.

The fourth stage involves interpreting the diagrams and calculations you have produced. This should lead to an indication of whether the hypothesis has been supported or not.

After completing the full cycle, it may be necessary to refine the original hypothesis and begin the cycle again.

The way you collect the data, and how you represent it, may depend on the type of data you want.

When data is first collected it is called **raw data**. Raw data is data before it has been sorted.

Data can be **primary data** or **secondary data**.
Primary data are data which are collected to investigate the hypothesis.
Secondary data are data which have already been collected, usually for another purpose.

Data can be **qualitative** or **quantitative**.
Qualitative data are not numerical (a quality). These data measure a quality such as taste or colour.
Quantitative data involve numbers of some kind.

Quantitative data can be **discrete** or **continuous**.
Discrete data means exact values such as number of people in a car. It is numerical data that can only take certain values.
Continuous data are numerical data that are always measurements, such as distance or time, that have to be rounded to be recorded. They can take any value.

Example: Draw a table and tick the correct boxes to show whether the following data are qualitative or quantitative, discrete or continuous, and primary or secondary.

  a Sammi collects information about hair colour from the internet.

  b Kaye measures the height of 100 people.

  c Ashad spots the numbers on the sides of trains in the station.

Solution:

Person	Qualitative	Quantitative	Discrete	Continuous	Primary	Secondary
Sammi	✓		✓			✓
Kaye		✓		✓	✓	
Ashad		✓	✓		✓	

AQA *Examiner's tip*

Many students do not know these words and what they mean.
They often appear in questions so it is important to learn them!

Data are collected to answer questions.

For example, how many miles can a Formula 1 racing car run on one set of tyres?

The **population** of tyres is all the tyres that are the same type.

At some point a **sample** of the tyres will have been tested.

A sample is a small part of the population.

Information about the sample should be true for the population.

The **sample size** is important.

The bigger the sample then the more reliable the information.

So, the more tyres in the sample the more reliable the information.

However, it can be too expensive or time consuming to collect data on a very large sample.

You cannot test tyres then sell them.

Example: Ellie is investigating the question 'What is the average height of a Year 10 girl?'

   a   What is the population for her question?

   b   Give an advantage of a large sample.

   c   Give a disadvantage of a large sample.

Solution: **a**   All Year 10 girls (in the world).

   b   The larger the sample the more reliable the results.

   c   Trying to get too many results will be very time consuming.

Practise... 3.1 Types of data Ⓚ

G F E D C

D

1   Copy the table and tick the correct boxes for these data.

   a   Nat finds out the cost of a cruise holiday in the newspaper.

   b   Prita counts the number of red jelly babies in 100 bags.

   c   Niles records the weather at his home every day for one month.

Person	Qualitative	Quantitative	Discrete	Continuous	Primary	Secondary
Nat						
Prita						
Niles						

2   For each of the following say whether the data are quantitative or qualitative.

   a   The number of people at a cricket test match.

   b   The weights of newborn babies.

   c   How many cars a garage sells.

   d   Peoples' opinions of the latest Hollywood blockbuster.

   e   The best dog at Crufts.

   f   The time it takes to run the London Marathon.

   g   The colour of baked beans.

   h   How well your favourite football team played in their last match.

   i   The number of text messages received in a day.

3   For each of the following say whether the data are discrete or continuous.

   a   The number of votes for a party at a general election.

   b   The number of beans in a tin.

   c   The weight of recycling each household produces each week.

   d   How many people watch the Nine O'Clock news.

   e   How long it takes to walk to school.

   f   The number of sheep Farmer Angus has.

   g   The weights of Farmer Angus' sheep.

   h   The heights of Year 10 students in your school.

   i   The number of eggs laid by a hen.

4   Copy and complete the diagram by connecting the statements to their proper description. Use a different colour for each type of data.

The first one has been done for you.

| Lengths of fish caught in a competition |
| Number of goals scored by a football team |
| Ages of teachers at a school |
| Favourite colours in the tutor group |
| Number of sweets in a bag |
| Favourite type of music |
| Person's foot length |
| Person's shoe size |
| Cost of stamps |
| Best player in the Wales rugby team |

| Quantitative and discrete |
| Qualitative |
| Quantitative and continuous |

5   For the questionnaire opposite, copy the details down and then identify whether the information requested is:

   • quantitative and discrete

   • quantitative and continuous

   • qualitative.

Questionnaire

Age (years)	
Gender (M/F)	
Height (cm)	
Hand span (cm)	
Arm span (cm)	
Foot length (cm)	
Eye colour	
No. of brothers	
No. of sisters	
House number	
Favourite pet	

6   **a**   What is a sample?

   b   Why are samples taken rather than looking at the whole population?

   c   Give two reasons why a sample should not be too large.

⚠ 7   Write down some:

   a   qualitative data about a jumper someone has knitted for you

   b   quantitative discrete data about the football team you support

   c   quantitative continuous data about the launch of a space rocket

   d   primary data you might collect about your maths homework

   e   secondary data you might collect about keeping a pet rat.

8   A newspaper says that the majority of people support the removal of toll charges from the Humber Bridge.

The newspaper based their statement on some data. How do you think they obtained these data – from a sample or the whole population?

Explain your answer.

9   A company produces energy-saving light bulbs.

They claim each bulb uses 90% less energy in its lifetime compared to traditional bulbs.

Explain how and why sampling will have been used in testing this claim.

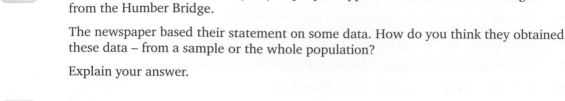

Learn... 3.2 Data collection methods

Writing a good questionnaire

One method of obtaining data is to ask people questions using a **questionnaire**.

Surveys often use questionnaires to find out information.

Questions can be **open** or **closed**.

Open questions allow for any response to be made.

Closed questions control the responses by using options.

It is important that questionnaires:

- are easy to understand
- are short and do not ask for irrelevant information
- give option boxes where possible
- do not have overlap or omissions in them where options boxes are used
- are not biased (such as 'Do you agree that …?')
- avoid asking for personal information unless vital to the survey
- are tested before being used to show up errors or problems (this is called a **pilot survey**).

Example: A shop manager wants to know the age of his customers.

He considers using one of these questions in a questionnaire.

> **Q1.** How old are you?   Answer_____

or

> **Q2.** Tick the box that contains your age.
>   20 or under   20 – 40   over 50
>   ☐   ☐   ☐

a   What problems might there be with these questions?

b   Write an improved question.

Solution: **a**   Q1 is an open question so all kinds of different answers (responses) can be given. e.g. $18\frac{1}{2}$, 45, not telling you, over 50
This would make the data very difficult to organise.

Also people may not wish to give their exact age.

Q2 is a closed question so people are more likely to answer it. However, the option boxes are badly designed.

For example:

The groups overlap. If you are 20 which box do you tick?

Some ages are missing. There is no box for people in their 40s.

The groups are quite wide so details are vague about the ages.

b   Tick the box that contains your age.

☐   ☐   ☐   ☐

under 20   20–39   40–59   60 or over

Other methods of collecting data

Surveys (and questionnaires) can be carried out in many ways.

Here are the most common.

Each method has advantages and disadvantages.

Method	Description	Advantages	Disadvantages
Face to face interviews/ telephone surveys	This is the most common method of collecting data and involves asking questions of the interviewee.	Can explain more complex questions if necessary. Interviewer is likely to be more consistent when they record the responses. More likely to get responses than with postal or email surveys.	Takes a lot of time and can be expensive. The interviewer may cause bias by influencing answers. The interviewee is more likely to lie or to refuse to answer a question.
Postal or email surveys	These surveys involve people being selected and sent a questionnaire.	The interviewees can take their time answering and give more thought to the answer. The possibility of interviewer bias is avoided. The cost is usually low.	Low response rates which may cause bias. Can take a long time. Different people might interpret questions in different ways when giving their answers.
Observation	This means observing the situation directly. For example, counting cars at a motorway junction or observing someone to see what shopping they buy. It can take place over a short or a long period of time.	Usually can be relied upon as those being watched do not know they are being observed and so act naturally. Often has little cost involved.	For some experiments, people may act differently because they know they are being observed. Takes a lot of time. Outside influences out of your control can affect the observations. Different observers can view the same thing but record it differently.
Controlled experiment	An experiment is more general than you might think and is not just for science. For example, timing cars along a particular piece of road is an experiment.	Results should be reliable. Repeats of the same conditions are possible if more data is needed.	Getting the right conditions for the experiment may be difficult, costly or time consuming. The experiment may need special equipment or expertise.
Data logging	A 'dumb' machine collects data automatically such as in a shop or car park entrance. The machine could then prevent more cars trying to enter an already full car park.	Once set up, machines can work without needing human resources. Data collection is continued for as long as required.	Machines breaking down can cause problems. As the machine is 'dumb' there is no detail in the data collection.

Practise...   3.2 Data collection methods (k!)   G F E D C

D

1   The following questions are taken from different surveys.

Write down one criticism of each question.

Rewrite the question in a more suitable form.

a   How many hours of TV do you watch each week?

Less than one hour ☐   More than one hour ☐

b   What is your favourite football team?

Real Madrid ☐   Luton Town ☐

c   How do you spend your leisure time? (You can only tick one box.)

Doing homework ☐   Playing sport ☐   Reading ☐

Computer games ☐   On the internet ☐   Sleeping ☐

d   You do like football, don't you?

Yes ☐   No ☐

e   How much do you earn each year?

Less than £10 000 ☐   £10 000 to £20 000 ☐   More than £20 000 ☐

f   How often do you go to the cinema?

Rarely ☐   Sometimes ☐   Often ☐

g   Do you or do you not travel by taxi?

Yes ☐   No ☐

h   I hate dogs. What do you think?

So do I ☐   They are OK ☐   Not sure ☐

2   Peter is writing questions for a research task.

This is one question from Peter's questionnaire.

> Skateboarding is an excellent pastime. Don't you agree? Tick one of the boxes.
> Strongly agree ☐   Agree ☐   Don't know ☐

Write down two criticisms of Peter's question.

D
C

3   Write down the data collection method being used in each of these situations giving one advantage and one disadvantage of each method.

a   A machine counts entry to a nightclub to prevent it becoming overcrowded.

b   Jez fills in some questions on his PC about his mobile phone contract.

c   Doctor Jekyll records blood pressure rates of people watching horror films.

d   Annie is stopped by a person with a clipboard on the High Street asking about perfume.

e   Iona records where students sit in a classroom the first time they enter it.

C

4   Give **two** reasons why a pilot survey might be carried out.

5 For each of the following situations write a single:

   a closed question   **b** open question.

      i To find out whether an adult is married or not

      ii To find out the cost of getting the train to Glasgow

   c Explain, for each situation, whether your open or closed question is better for finding out the desired information.

6 Write a questionnaire which could be used to find out:

   a where students have been on holiday in the last two years

   b who likes Wayne Rooney

   c the cost of newspapers bought by student families.

> **AQA** *Examiner's tip*
> Remember to allow for all possible responses in a question.

Learn... 3.3 Organising data k!

Once you have collected data, you need to organise them.

Before being organised in any way, data are called raw data.

The simplest way of organising data is in a **tally chart**.

Each item is shown as a single stroke or 'tally' like this |

Five items are shown as four strokes with a line through like this ||||

A frequency column can then be used to give the total of the tallies for each value or group of values.

A table like this with total frequencies is called a **frequency table**.

Example: k! The following information, collected from newspapers, shows the numbers of words in sentences.

16	22	14	12	19	23	18	21	24	29	17
22	17	11	15	18	19	20	22	15	17	18
25	16	21	20	19	15	12	14	8	11	19

Show this information in a tally chart.

Solution: There are too many different values to have a row for each one, so they need to be tallied in groups.

Step 1 Use groups for the data

When choosing groups it is best to have between four and eight groups of the same size.

The tally chart before any tallying could then look like this.

Number of words	Tally	Frequency
5–9		
10–14		
15–19		
20–24		
25–29		

The first group of 5–9 was chosen because the lowest value is 8.

The last group of 25–29 was chosen because the highest value is 29.

The range of each group (a five number spread) was chosen to give between four and eight group rows in the table.

Note – there are other equally good answers, e.g. 6–10, 11–15 and so on.

Step 2 Tally the data into the groups

Now go through the data one by one and tally the values in the chart as shown below.

For example, the first value is 16 so a tally is made in the 15–19 row.

Number of words	Tally	Frequency
5–9	I	1
10–14	IIII I	6
15–19	IIII IIII IIII	15
20–24	IIII IIII	9
25–29	II	2

Step 3 The tallies are counted for each group

Count the tallies for each group and put the total in the frequency column.

Step 4 Check frequency total

To check that you have not made any errors add up the frequency values.
Check this against the number of data values in the data set.

There were 33 data values given in the newspaper data set.

Frequency total $= 1 + 6 + 15 + 9 + 2 = 33$ ✓

Sometimes when collecting data you need to design a **data collection sheet** or **observation sheet**.

These can be very similar to a tally chart but can also be like the one in the following example.

Example: Quinlan is collecting data about the types of vehicles passing his house.

He wants to see if there are differences between weekdays and weekends.

Design an observation sheet that Quinlan could use.

Solution: Here is one possible answer.

	Car	Bus	Lorry	Bicycle	Other
Weekday					
Weekend					

AQA **Examiner's tip**

In examinations students often forget to include a section for 'other'. Data collection sheets must allow for all possible outcomes in the situation that you are observing.

The table in the example above is an example of a **two-way table**.

Two-way tables are used to show more than one aspect of the data at the same time (time of week and type of vehicle).

Two-way tables can show lots of information at once.

Example: Students in a school were asked whether they had school dinners or packed lunches. Their results are shown in the table below.

	Boys	Girls
School dinner	24	16
Packed lunch	12	32

Write down nine facts that can be obtained from this two-way table.

Solution: 24 boys have school dinner.

16 girls have school dinner.

12 boys have packed lunch.

32 girls have packed lunch.

40 (24 + 16) students have school dinner.

44 (12 + 32) students have packed lunch.

36 (24 + 12) boys have either school dinner or packed lunch.

48 (16 + 32) girls have either school dinner or packed lunch.

84 (24 + 16 + 12 + 32) students have either school dinner or packed lunch.

Practise...   3.3 Organising data k!

G F E D C

1   Use the following information to copy and complete the tally chart.

```
3   2   2   1   3   4   0   1   3
0   2   1   1   4   3   2   2   1
3   2   3   1   1   0   4   3   2
2   0   1   0   1   1   0   2   3
```

Number	Tally	Frequency
0		
1		
2		
3		
4		

G

2   The tally chart in Question 1 shows the number of bedrooms in properties advertised in a newspaper. Use your table to provide the following data.

a   How many properties were surveyed altogether?

b   How many properties had three bedrooms?

3   The following information shows the marks obtained by a class in a test.

```
15   17   23   25   22   18   17   14   12   10   14   18   21   22
23   17   14   10   11   16   18   21   21   22   19   14   13   21
```

Use the information to copy and complete the tally chart below.

Number	Tally	Frequency
10–13		
14–17		
18–21		
22–25		

F

4   The tally chart shows the heights (in centimetres to the nearest centimetre) of bushes in a garden centre.

The interval $10 < h \leqslant 15$ includes all heights from 10 cm to 15 cm but not including 10 cm ⟶

Number	Tally	Frequency
$5 < h \leqslant 10$	ЖТ |||	
$10 < h \leqslant 15$	ЖТ ЖТ	
$15 < h \leqslant 20$	ЖТ ||	
$20 < h \leqslant 25$	ЖТ	

Copy and complete the table and use it to answer the following questions.

a   How many bushes were surveyed in the garden centre?

b   How many bushes had heights between 10 cm and 15 cm?

c   How many bushes had heights above 15 cm?

D

5 The two-way table shows information about gender and wearing glasses.

	Boys	Girls
Glasses	8	17
No glasses	15	24

Use the table to answer the following questions.

a How many people wear glasses?

b How many girls were in the survey?

c How many boys do not wear glasses?

d What method of data collection could have been used to obtain these data?

6 The table shows the different animals on a farm.

	Sheep	Cattle	Pigs
Male	80		90
Female		70	

The farmer has:
- 130 sheep in total
- 340 male animals
- 600 animals in total.

Copy and complete the table

7 Mike thinks the weather is often better in the morning than the afternoon.

Design an observation sheet to collect data to investigate this.

8 A school has 100 students. 52 boys play football.

Of the 33 girls, $\frac{6}{11}$ play football and the rest do not.

Copy and complete the two-way table.

	Play football	Do not play football
Boys		
Girls		

9 The two-way table shows the price of holidays.

Prices per person per week for Costa Packet

	7th April to 5th June	6th June to 21st July	22nd July to 5th Sept
Adult	£124	£168	£215
Child (6–16 years)	£89	£120	£199
Child (0–5 years)	Free	£12	£50

The Brown family consists of 2 adults and 2 children aged 3 and 12 years.

They have a maximum of £500 to spend on a one week holiday at Costa Packet.

a On which dates could they go on their holiday?

b Mr Brown says that if they save up another £200 they could have a two week holiday at Costa Packet.

Is he correct?

3 Assess

1 Use the following information to complete the tally chart.

3 1 2 4 3 2 0 2 3 3
2 0 4 2 2 3 1 1 0 3
2 1 1 3 2 4 2 1 0 0
3 4 3 2 2

Number	Tally	Frequency
0		
1		
2		
3		
4		

2 The following information shows the marks obtained in a test.

16 18 19 23 24 25 22 15 16 11 10 19 22 25
25 18 10 15 16 19 17 25 23 20 18 12 16 18

Use this information to complete the tally chart below.

Number	Tally	Frequency
10–13		
14–17		
18–21		
22–25		

3 In a survey, 40 adults are asked if they are left-handed or right-handed.

	Men	Women
Left-handed	5	8
Right-handed	19	8

Use the table above to answer the following questions.

a How many men are in the survey?

b How many of the 40 adults are right-handed?

c What fraction of those asked are right-handed men?

d What percentage of women asked are left-handed?

4 Some teachers are asked to choose their favourite snack, chocolate or sweets. Some of the results are shown in this table.

	Chocolate	Sweets
Male	24	
Female	16	

a A total of 50 male teachers are asked and 30 teachers choose sweets. Copy and complete the table.

b How many females are asked?

c How many teachers are asked altogether?

d What fraction of the teachers who prefer chocolate are female? Give your answer in its simplest form.

D **5** **a** Criticise each of the following questionnaire questions.

    i How many hours of television have you watched in the last two months?

    ii Do you or do you not watch news programmes?

b Criticise each of the following questionnaire questions and suggest better alternatives to find out the same information.

    i What do you think about our new improved fruit juice?

    ii How much do you earn?

    iii Do you or do you not agree with the new bypass?

    iv Would you prefer to sit in a non-smoking area?

    v How often do you have a shower?

C **6** Briefly explain a good method for collecting data in each of these situations.

a The average weight of sheep on a farm with 1000 sheep.

b The favourite building of people in your town.

c The average amount of time spent on homework each week by students in your school.

d The average hand span of students in a school.

e The views of villagers on a new shopping centre.

f Information on voting intentions at a general election.

g The number of people entering a shop in the month of December.

7 The owners of a small shop claim to have the cheapest prices for fruit and vegetables in a small town.

Discuss how this could be tested by explaining how the full data-handling cycle could be used in this investigation.

8 Mr and Mrs Khan and their three children (Ali aged 14, Ravi aged 12 and Sabina aged 3) are planning a two-week-long holiday to Spain. The table shows the cost:

	May	June	July
Adult	£152	£174	£225
Child (5–16)	£120	£140	£209
Child (under 5)	Free	£25	£30

How much cheaper is it if they go to Spain in May rather than in June?

AQA Examination-style questions 🌑

1   **a**   30 students from Year 7 are asked how they travel to school. Their replies, walk (W), bus (B) or car (C) are shown below.

C   C   B   W   B   W   C   B   W   C

B   B   W   W   W   C   W   C   C   B

W   W   B   W   B   W   B   W   W   C

i   Copy and complete the tally column and the frequency column in the table.   *(3 marks)*

	Tally	Frequency
Walk (W)		
Bus (B)		
Car (C)		
Total		30

ii   Which reply is the most common?   *(1 mark)*

iii   What fraction of the students travel by bus?   *(1 mark)*

b   30 students from Year 11 are also asked how they travel to school. Their results are shown in the table.

	Frequency
Walk (W)	13
Bus (B)	14
Car (C)	3
Total	30

Compare how Year 7 and Year 11 travel to school.

i   Write down **one** difference.   *(1 mark)*

ii   Write down **one** similarity.   *(1 mark)*

(AQA 2008)

4 Percentages

Objectives

Examiners would normally expect students who get these grades to be able to:

F

understand that percentage means 'number of parts per 100'

change between percentages and fractions or decimals

E

compare percentages, fractions and decimals

work out a percentage of a given quantity

D

increase or decrease by a given percentage

express one quantity as a percentage of another

C

work out a percentage increase or decrease.

Try this!

Breakfast bits

Do you like bits in your orange juice?

A survey of British people found that:
- 15% won't touch orange juice with bits in it
- 7% won't have it without bits
- 7% won't eat the bits in marmalade or jam.

We have other loves and hates at breakfast time:
- 25% won't eat cereal that has gone soggy
- 14% demand to have matching cutlery
- 7% insist that the crusts are cut off their toast.

Carry out a survey to find out what students in your class love or hate at breakfast time. Surveys often give results in percentages. After working through this chapter you will be able to present the results of your own surveys in percentages.

Key terms

percentage	discount
amount	deposit
Value Added Tax (VAT)	balance
rate	credit
depreciation	interest
principal	

You should already know:

✔ place values in decimals

✔ how to put decimals in order of size

✔ how to simplify fractions

✔ how to write a fraction as a decimal and vice versa.

Learn... 4.1 Percentages, fractions and decimals

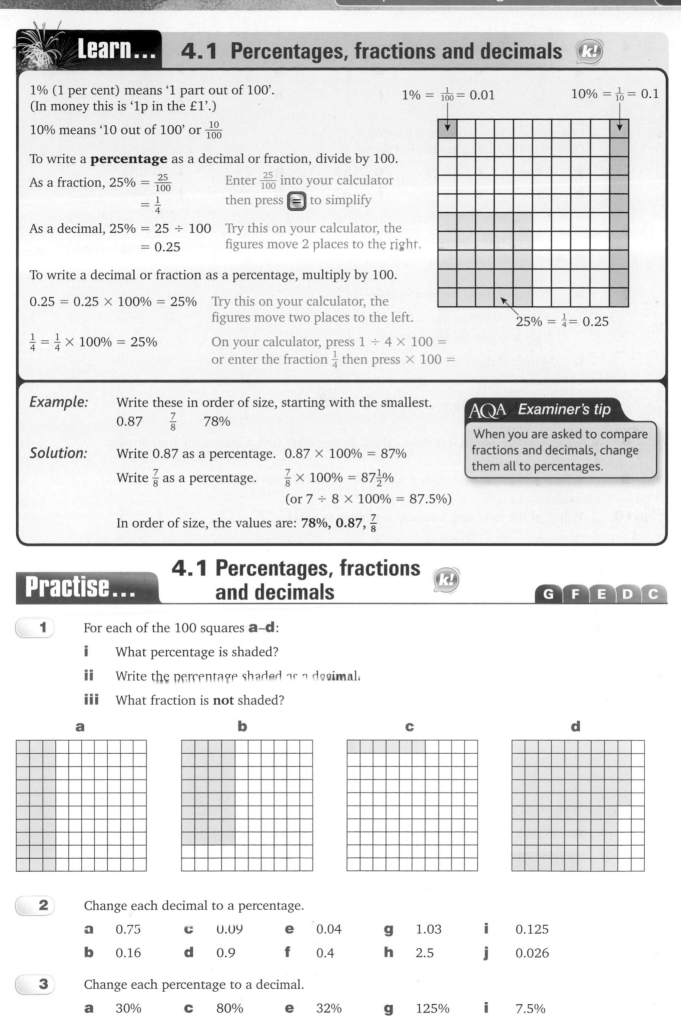

1% (1 per cent) means '1 part out of 100'.
(In money this is '1p in the £1'.)

10% means '10 out of 100' or $\frac{10}{100}$

To write a **percentage** as a decimal or fraction, divide by 100.

As a fraction, 25% = $\frac{25}{100}$ Enter $\frac{25}{100}$ into your calculator

= $\frac{1}{4}$ then press = to simplify

As a decimal, 25% = 25 ÷ 100   Try this on your calculator, the

= 0.25   figures move 2 places to the right.

To write a decimal or fraction as a percentage, multiply by 100.

0.25 = 0.25 × 100% = 25%   Try this on your calculator, the
figures move two places to the left.

$\frac{1}{4}$ = $\frac{1}{4}$ × 100% = 25%   On your calculator, press 1 ÷ 4 × 100 =
or enter the fraction $\frac{1}{4}$ then press × 100 =

1% = $\frac{1}{100}$ = 0.01   10% = $\frac{1}{10}$ = 0.1

25% = $\frac{1}{4}$ = 0.25

Example: Write these in order of size, starting with the smallest.

0.87 $\frac{7}{8}$ 78%

Solution: Write 0.87 as a percentage.   0.87 × 100% = 87%

Write $\frac{7}{8}$ as a percentage. $\frac{7}{8}$ × 100% = $87\frac{1}{2}$%

(or 7 ÷ 8 × 100% = 87.5%)

In order of size, the values are: **78%, 0.87,** $\frac{7}{8}$

AQA   *Examiner's tip*

When you are asked to compare
fractions and decimals, change
them all to percentages.

Practise... 4.1 Percentages, fractions and decimals

G F E D C

1   For each of the 100 squares **a–d**:

i   What percentage is shaded?

ii   Write the percentage shaded as a decimal.

iii   What fraction is **not** shaded?

a   **b**   **c**   **d**

2   Change each decimal to a percentage.

a   0.75   **c**   0.09   **e**   0.04   **g**   1.03   **i**   0.125

b   0.16   **d**   0.9   **f**   0.4   **h**   2.5   **j**   0.026

3   Change each percentage to a decimal.

a   30%   **c**   80%   **e**   32%   **g**   125%   **i**   7.5%

b   47%   **d**   8%   **f**   3%   **h**   375%   **j**   62.5%

G

F

F

4 Change each fraction to a percentage.

a $\frac{27}{100}$ **c** $\frac{9}{10}$ **e** $\frac{1}{5}$ **g** $\frac{4}{5}$ **i** $\frac{9}{20}$

b $\frac{3}{100}$ **d** $\frac{7}{20}$ **f** $\frac{3}{4}$ **h** $\frac{16}{25}$ **j** $\frac{3}{8}$

5 Change each percentage to a fraction.
Give each fraction in its simplest form.

a 49%   **c** 36%   **e** 5%   **g** 2%   **i** 40%

b 70%   **d** 65%   **f** 60%   **h** 8%   **j** 24%

E

6 Write these in order of size, smallest first.

a $\frac{1}{5}$, 0.3, 25%   **b** 72%, $\frac{3}{4}$, 0.7   **c** 0.6, 58%, $\frac{13}{20}$

7 **a** Which of these are greater than $\frac{1}{2}$?

47%, 0.054, $\frac{4}{7}$, 8.5%, 0.62

Give a reason for your answer.

b Which of these are less than $\frac{1}{4}$?

24%, 0.3, $\frac{2}{9}$, 40%, 0.09

Give a reason for your answer.

D

8 Tina says that 34% is less than a third. Is she right? Give a reason for your answer.

9 Tom says that five-eighths is 0.625%. What mistake has he made?

⚠ 10 Which of the following fractions is nearest to 50%?

$\frac{4}{10}$ $\frac{9}{20}$ $\frac{14}{30}$ $\frac{19}{40}$

Show how you decided.

⚠ 11 **a** Copy the number square.

b Change each fraction to a percentage.

c Write the percentage answer with three digits down the centre.

d Use your other percentage answers to fill the rest of the square.

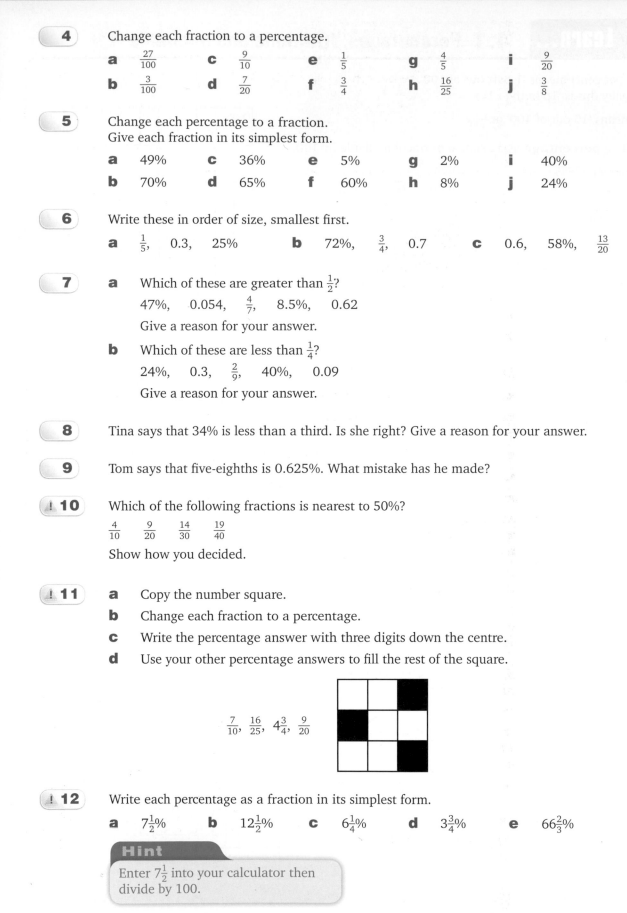

$\frac{7}{10}$, $\frac{16}{25}$, $4\frac{3}{4}$, $\frac{9}{20}$

⚠ 12 Write each percentage as a fraction in its simplest form.

a $7\frac{1}{2}\%$ **b** $12\frac{1}{2}\%$ **c** $6\frac{1}{4}\%$ **d** $3\frac{3}{4}\%$ **e** $66\frac{2}{3}\%$

Hint

Enter $7\frac{1}{2}$ into your calculator then divide by 100.

❓ 13 Amir, Emma and Duncan have saved some money.

Emma has saved 83% of the **amount** Amir has saved.

Duncan has saved $\frac{33}{40}$ of the amount Amir has saved.

Who has saved the most, Emma or Duncan?

Give a reason for your answer.

Learn...   4.2 Finding a percentage of a quantity

To find a percentage of a quantity:
- **find 1% by dividing by 100**
- then **multiply by the percentage** you need.

To find a percentage of a quantity using a decimal multiplier.
- To find 1% you multiply by 0.01 (1 ÷ 100)
- To find 10% you multiply by 0.10 (10 ÷ 100)
- To find 63% you multiply by 0.63 etc (63 ÷ 100).

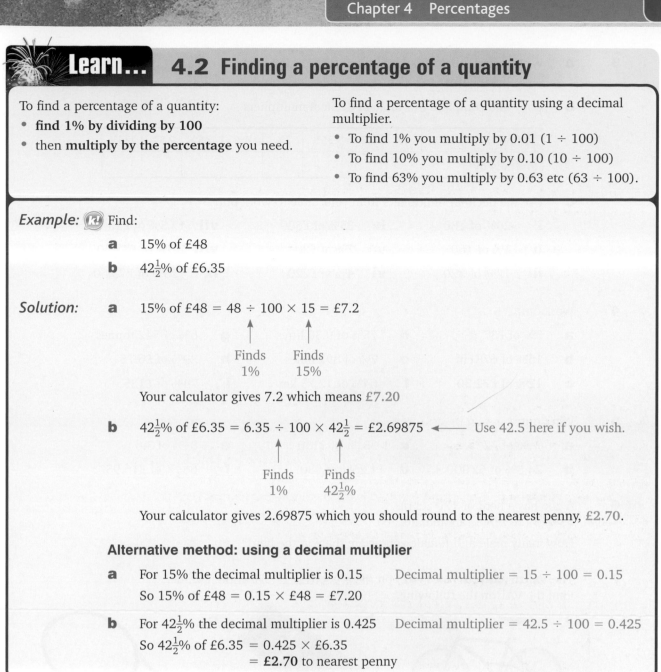

Example: Find:

   a   15% of £48

   b $42\frac{1}{2}$% of £6.35

Solution: **a**   15% of £48 = 48 ÷ 100 × 15 = £7.2

                              ↑ Finds 1%   ↑ Finds 15%

   Your calculator gives 7.2 which means £7.20

   b $42\frac{1}{2}$% of £6.35 = 6.35 ÷ 100 × $42\frac{1}{2}$ = £2.69875   ←— Use 42.5 here if you wish.

                              ↑ Finds 1%   ↑ Finds $42\frac{1}{2}$%

   Your calculator gives 2.69875 which you should round to the nearest penny, £2.70.

   Alternative method: using a decimal multiplier

   a   For 15% the decimal multiplier is 0.15   Decimal multiplier = 15 ÷ 100 = 0.15
         So 15% of £48 = 0.15 × £48 = £7.20

   b   For $42\frac{1}{2}$% the decimal multiplier is 0.425   Decimal multiplier = 42.5 ÷ 100 = 0.425
         So $42\frac{1}{2}$% of £6.35 = 0.425 × £6.35
                           = **£2.70** to nearest penny

Practise...   4.2 Finding a percentage of a quantity   G F E D C

F

1   Work out:

   a   25% of £140   **c**   20% of £190   **e**   70% of £280

   b   75% of £3000   **d**   30% of £8400   **f**   95% of £80

   Use a different method to check your answers.

2   Work out:

   a   15% of 240 m   **c**   32% of 4500 litres   **e**   23% of 800 g

   b   56% of 500 kg   **d**   45% of 80 km   **f**   74% of 250 ml

   Use a different method to check your answers.

3

a Write down the decimal multiplier for working out 20% of a quantity.

> **Hint**
>
> Decimal multiplier = 20 ÷ 100 (for 20%)

b Copy and complete this table of decimal multipliers.

To find	20%	1%	12%	35%	7%	4%	17.5%	2.5%	125%
Multiply by									

c Use the decimal multipliers from your table to work out:

i 20% of 150   **iv** 35% of £500   **vii** 17.5% of £150

ii 1% of 160   **v** 7% of £20   **viii** 2.5% of £32.50

iii 12% of 320   **vi** 4% of £220   **ix** 125% of £25.60

4 Work out:

a 5% of £37   **d** 75% of 9.36 litres   **g** 6% of 542 tonnes

b 15% of 678 cm   **e** 7% of 892 miles   **h** 29% of £6.75

c 12% of £72.50   **f** 64% of 12.75 km   **i** 74% of £135

5 Work out:

a $7\frac{1}{2}$% of 72   **c** $33\frac{1}{3}$% of 3150   **e** $8\frac{3}{4}$% of 3.6

b 24.5% of 62 000   **d** 1.25% of 980   **f** $66\frac{2}{3}$% of £16.95

6 A zoo has a herd of 120 zebras.
55% of the zebras are female.

How many male and female zebras are there in the herd?

7 The **Value Added Tax (VAT)** on these goods is 17.5% of their value.
Find the VAT on the following.

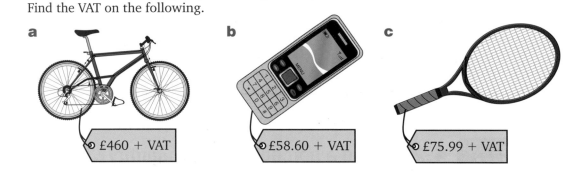

a £460 + VAT   **b** £58.60 + VAT   **c** £75.99 + VAT

8 Gas and electricity companies charge 5% VAT on their bills.
Find the VAT on each of these bills.

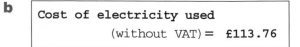

a
```
Gas you've used
(without VAT) =  £217.62
```

b
```
Cost of electricity used
          (without VAT) =  £113.76
```

9 Katie says '40% of £18 is seven pounds and two pence.'
Is she correct?

Explain your answer.

10 Tom has £2200.

He gives 15% to his son and 30% to his daughter.

He keeps the rest.

How much does Tom keep?

You **must** show your working.

11 Currently, the population of the UK is approximately 61 million.

About 13% of the population is between 5 and 15 years old.

By 2031 the population is expected to rise to 71 million.

About 12.4% of the population is expected to be between 5 and 15 years old.

How many more children between 5 and 15 years old are there expected to be in 2031?

12 In 2009 a TV set cost £650 **excluding** VAT.

During 2009 the **rate** of VAT was reduced from 17.5% to 15%

How much less was the cost of the TV set **including** VAT after the VAT rate was reduced?

13 Amie, Ben, Carrie, Dave, Emma and Fergus share £200 between them.

Amie gets 10% of the £200.

Ben gets 20% of what is left.

Carrie gets 30% of what is left after Amie and Ben take their share.

Dave gets 40% of what is left after Amie, Ben and Carrie take their share.

Emma and Fergus share the remainder.

Who gets the most?

14 Last year, 10% of the animals seen by a vet are cats.

The vet sees twice as many dogs as cats.

Last year, the vet saw 210 animals that were **not** cats or dogs.

How many animals did the vet see?

Learn... 4.3 Increasing or decreasing by a percentage

To increase or decrease by a given percentage:
- **Find 1% by dividing by 100**.
- Then **multiply by the percentage** you need.
- For a % increase, add to the original quantity. For a % decrease, subtract from the original quantity.

An alternative method is to use a decimal multiplier.
- Write the new quantity as a % of the original quantity.
- Convert this % to a decimal **multiplier**.
- Multiply by the original quantity

Example: **a** Increase £84 by 20%   **b** Decrease 75 800 by 12.5%

Solution: **a** 20% of £84 $= \frac{84}{100} \times 20$

$= 16.8$

New amount $= 16.8 + 84$
$= £100.80$

b 12.5% of 75 800 $= \frac{12.5}{100} \times 75\,800$

$= 9475$

New amount $= 75\,800 - 9475$
$= 66\,325$

AQA *Examiner's tip*

Don't forget to add a zero to complete the pence.

Does your calculator have an (ANS) key?
You can use it here.

Alternative method: using a decimal multiplier

a New amount $= 100\% + 20\% = 120\%$
The multiplier $= 1.20$
New amount $= 1.2 \times 84$
$= £100.80$

b New amount $= 100\% - 12.5\% = 87.5\%$
The multiplier $= 0.875$
New amount $= 0.875 \times 75\,800$
$= 66\,325$

Practise... 4.3 Increasing or decreasing by a percentage 🔑 G F E D C

D

1
  a   Increase £40 by 25%   **c**   Decrease £375 by 40%

  b   Increase £35 000 by 20%   **d**   Decrease £7.60 by 75%

Use a different method to check your answers.

2
  a   Increase 120 m by 50%   **c**   Decrease 8 miles by 15%

  b   Increase 70 kg by 30%   **d**   Decrease 62.5 litres by 18%

Use a different method to check your answers.

3
  a   Increase £35.40 by 29%   **c**   Decrease £75 by 5%

  b   Increase £260 by 12.5%   **d**   Decrease £49.99 by $33\frac{1}{3}$%

4
  a   Write down the decimal multiplier for increasing a quantity by 20%

  b   Copy and complete these tables.

To increase by	20%	40%	8%	3.5%
Multiply by				

To decrease by	20%	40%	8%	3.5%
Multiply by				

> **Hint**
>
> This is how you work out the decimal multiplier for increasing a quantity by 20%
>
> Decimal multiplier = (100 + 20) ÷ 100

  c   Use the decimal multipliers from your table to work out the following.

    i   150 increased by 20%   **v**   150 decreased by 20%

    ii   160 increased by 40%   **vi**   160 decreased by 40%

    iii 320 increased by 8%   **vii** 320 decreased by 8%

    iv 250 increased by 3.5%   **viii** 250 decreased by 3.5%

5
The cost of a rail journey is £78.50.

What is the new price after a 4% increase?

Use a different method to check your answers.

> **AQA Examiner's tip**
>
> It is a good idea to always **check** your answers. One way of doing this is to use a different method if you know one.

6
The table gives the original prices of some clothes.

The shop reduces these prices by 30% in a sale.

Find the new prices.

Item	Original price
Trousers	£48.90
Shirt	£29.50
Jumper	£35.95
Gloves	£17.99

7
Gemma bought a car last year for £8900.

It has **depreciated** in value by 15%

What is it worth now?

> **Hint**
>
> Depreciation is a fall in value.

D
C

8
Paul opens a building society account with £2500.

The interest rate is 6% per year.

What is the amount in the account after:

> **Hint**
>
> £2500 is the **principal**.

  a   1 year   **b**   2 years

9 This coat costs £95.50 before the sale.

Work out the price of the coat in the sale.

SALE
15% off

10 The prices of each of these items are given **excluding** VAT.
Find the cost of each item **including** VAT at the rate given.

a
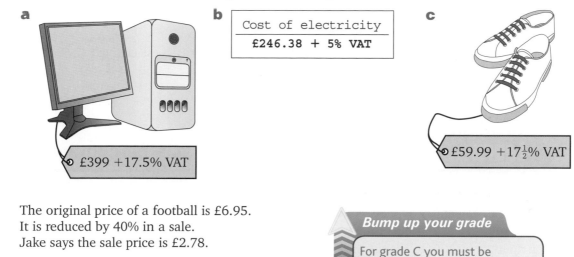
£399 +17.5% VAT

b
Cost of electricity
£246.38 + 5% VAT

c
£59.99 +17½% VAT

11 The original price of a football is £6.95.
It is reduced by 40% in a sale.
Jake says the sale price is £2.78.

Is he correct? Explain your answer.

Bump up your grade

For grade C you must be able to explain errors.

12 A zoo puts up its prices by 5%.
In the first week after the increase, it gives a **discount** of 5%.
Sunita says the cost will be back to the old price.

Do you agree? Explain your answer.

13 The table shows the salaries of some of a company's employees.

Job	Number of employees	Salary (per year)
Clerical assistant	5	£15 400
Factory worker	25	£16 900
Warehouse worker	8	£17 500
Delivery driver	4	£19 750

The company is discussing these two offers for a pay rise with the employees.

Offer 1
A salary increase of £350 for all employees

Offer 2
A 2% salary increase

a Tina and Afzal are clerical assistants.
Tina says Offer 1 gives her a bigger increase. Afzal disagrees.
Who is correct?
Give a reason for your answer.

b Which offer is best for each of the other workers?
Give a reason for each of your answers.

c Overall, which offer would cost the company less money?

14   Sally wants to buy a drum kit priced at £495.

She pays a **deposit** of £100.

There are two ways she can pay the rest of the price (the **balance**).

> **EasyPay Option**
> 7.5% **credit** charge on the balance
> 6 equal monthly payments
>
> **PayLess Option**
> 2.5% **interest** added each month to the amount owed
> pay £50 per month until the balance is paid off
> (In the last month Sally will only pay the remaining balance, not a full £50.)

Investigate these two options and advise Sally which one is best.

Would your advice be different if EasyPay charged 8% or PayLess charged 1.5% each month?

Learn... 4.4 Writing one quantity as a percentage of another

To write one quantity as a percentage of another:

- Divide the first quantity by the second. This gives you a decimal (or write the first quantity as a fraction of the second).
- Then multiply by 100, to change the decimal or fraction to a percentage.

Example: Write 80 pence as a percentage of £5.

Solution: $\frac{80}{500} \times 100 = 16$

     £5 = 500p

so 80 pence is 16% of £5.   You can work in £ if you prefer.

         $0.80 \div 5 \times 100 = 16$

> **AQA Examiner's tip**
> The quantities must be in the **same units**.

Example: In one month, 108 baby boys and 96 baby girls are born in a maternity hospital.

What percentage of the babies are boys?

What percentage are girls?

> **AQA Examiner's tip**
> You must write each number as a percentage of the **total**.

Solution: The total number of babies = 108 + 96 = 204

Percentage that are boys = $\frac{108}{204} \times 100 = 52.9\%$ (to 1 d.p.)

Percentage that are girls = 100% − 52.9% = 47.1% (to 1 d.p.)

or 96 ÷ 204 × 100 = 47.1%. Then use 47.1% + 52.9% = 100% to check.

Example: The table shows the marks students get in a test.

   a   What percentage of students get less than 10?

   b   Students must get 20 or more to pass.

      i   What percentage of students pass?

      ii   What percentage of students fail?

Marks	Frequency
0–9	4
10–19	7
20–29	9
30–39	8
40–49	4

Solution:
   a   The total number of students = $4 + 7 + 9 + 8 + 4 = 32$
           4 out of 32 students get less than 10

Divide by the total

           Percentage of students who get less than 10 = $4 \div 32 \times 100 = $ **12.5%**

                          or $\frac{4}{32} \times 100 = 12\frac{1}{2}\%$

   b   The number of students who get 20 or more = $9 + 8 + 4 = 21$

      i   Percentage of students who pass = $\frac{21}{32} \times 100 = $ **65.6%**

     ii   Percentage of students who fail = $100\% - 65.6\% = $ **34.4%**

         Alternatively: The number who fail = $32 - 21 = 11$ then $\frac{11}{32} \times 100 = 34.4\%$

Practise...
4.4 Writing one quantity as a percentage of another

G F E D C

When answers are not exact, round them to 1 decimal place.

1   Write:

   a   £32 as a percentage of £200   **d**   £325 as a percentage of £750

   b   25p as a percentage of 80p   **e**   65p as a percentage of £5.20

   c   28p as a percentage of £3.50   **f**   £18 500 as a percentage of £25 000

2   Express:

   a   24 kg as a percentage of 50 kg   **d**   850 cm as a percentage of 500 cm

   b   5 cm as a percentage of 200 cm   **e**   280 cm as a percentage of 250 cm

   c   250 g as a percentage of 500 g   **f**   87 000 as a percentage of 1 million

3   In a survey, 28 out of 40 people say they prefer butter to margarine.
      What percentage is this?

4   Out of 52 people who take a driving test, 34 pass.

   a   What percentage of the people pass?   **b**   What percentage of the people fail?

5   A class contains 15 boys and 17 girls.
      10 out of the boys in the class have school dinners.
      8 out of the girls in the class have school dinners.

   a   What percentage of the boys in the class has school dinners?

   b   What percentage of the girls in the class has school dinners?

   c   What percentage of the whole class has school dinners?

   d   What percentage of the whole class does not have school dinners?

6   The tally chart shows the hair colour of the students in a class.

Colour	Tally	Frequency
Blonde	ШΤ ШΤ	
Brown	ШΤ ШΤ |||	
Black	ШΤ	
Red	||	

Hint

Decide whether or not Ian is correct, then explain your decision.

The explanation can include calculations as well as a few words.

Ian looks at the tally chart and says 10% of the class has blonde hair.

Is Ian correct?

Explain your answer.

D

D
C

7 The table gives the colours of the cars in a car park.

Colour	Number of cars
Red	9
Black	6
White	8
Blue	4
Other	1

a What percentage of the cars are:

   i red

   ii black

   iii white

   iv blue

   v other colours?

b Describe one way you can check your answers to part **a**.

8 The table gives the ages of the people who go on an activity holiday.

Age	Frequency
0–9	1
10–19	36
20–39	33
40–59	8
60 and over	2

a What percentage of the people are under 20 years old?

b People who are 40 or over must pay for extra insurance.

What percentage of holidaymakers are 40 or over?

9 Write:

a 63 thousand as a percentage of 4 million

b £92.5 million as a percentage of £3 billion

c 745 cm as a percentage of 1.5 m

d 640 cm as a percentage of 0.2 km

e $1\frac{3}{4}$ hours as a percentage of 1 day.

Hint

1 billion = 1000 million

1 m = 100 cm

1 km = 1000 m

10 The surface area of the earth is 510 million km².

149 million km² is land and the rest is sea.

a What percentage of the earth's surface is land?

b What percentage of the earth's surface is sea?

11 A national travel survey asked people how often they cycled last year.

The results are shown in this table.

Cycled (number of times a week)	Number of people aged	
	5–15 years	16 years and over
once or more	1371	1576
less than once	792	2627
never	883	13 310

AQA Examiner's tip

When you are asked to compare sets of data with a different amount of data in each set, use percentages of the total amount of data in each set.

Use the data to compare the number of times that younger and older people cycle.

12 The table gives the number of students in a class who are left-handed and right-handed.

	Girls	Boys
Left-handed	38	49
Right-handed	402	421
Total	440	470

Use percentages to compare left-handedness between the genders.

Learn... 4.5 Percentage increase and decrease

To write an increase or decrease as a percentage:

- Find the increase or decrease.
- Divide the increase (or decrease) by the original amount.
- Multiply by 100 to change to a percentage.

Example: A rail fare goes up from £48 to £54. Find the percentage increase.

Solution: Fare increase = £54 − £48 = £6

Percentage increase = $\frac{6}{48} \times 100 = 12.5\%$

So the fare increases by 12.5%

> **AQA Examiner's tip**
> Remember to divide by the **original** amount.

Example: A worker takes $1\frac{1}{4}$ minutes to pack a box. After training he can do it in 50 seconds.

What is the percentage decrease in time?

> **AQA Examiner's tip**
> You must use the **same units**.

Solution: Before training, he takes 75 seconds ⟵ $1\frac{1}{4} \times 60 = 75$

Decrease in time = 75 − 50 = 25 seconds or $\frac{25}{75} \times 100 = 33\frac{1}{3}\%$

Percentage decrease = $\frac{25}{75} \times 100 = 33.3\%$ (to 1 d.p.)

Practise... 4.5 Percentage increase and decrease 📢 G F E D C

C

1 The price of a chocolate bar goes up from 80 pence to 86 pence.
Work out the percentage increase in the price of the chocolate bar.

> **Bump up your grade**
> For grade C you must be able to write an increase or decrease as a percentage.

2 A beekeeper had 25 hives last year. This year she has only 21 hives.

What is the percentage decrease in the number of hives?

3 A supermarket buys cauliflowers for 48 pence each.
It sells them for 85 pence each.
Work out the percentage profit.

The percentage profit is the percentage increase in price.

4 Mike buys a car for £18 700.
He sells it a year later for £16 300.
Work out his percentage loss.

The percentage loss is the percentage decrease in price.

C

5 The cost of a bus ride goes up from 95 pence to £1.05.

What is the percentage increase in the cost of a bus ticket?

6 A company employs fewer employees than 10 years ago.
The number of male workers has decreased from 8530 to 5380.
The number of female workers has decreased from 3150 to 1420.

a Work out the percentage fall in:

i the number of male workers

ii the number of female workers.

b Work out the percentage decrease for all workers.

7 The table gives the usual price and
sale price of a computer and printer.

	Usual price	Sale price
Computer	£549	£499
Printer	£89	£59

a Work out the percentage reduction in the price of:

i the computer

ii the printer.

b Work out the percentage reduction in the total price.

8 The rent of Sophie's flat has gone up from
£120 to £150 per week.
Sophie works out 30 ÷ 150 × 100
She says the rent has increased by 20%

a What mistake has she made?

b What is the actual percentage increase in Sophie's rent?

Bump up your grade

For grade C you must be able to explain why something is wrong.

9 The table shows differences between what we drink now and four years ago.

Drink	Average consumption per person, per week	
	Four years ago	Now
Fruit juice	280 ml	340 ml
Low calorie soft drinks	442 ml	508 ml
Other soft drinks	1.39 litres	1.18 litres
Beverages (e.g. tea, coffee)	56	56
Alcoholic drinks	763 ml	772 ml

Hint

Use percentage changes.

Compare these results.

10 The table gives the UK population in millions.

Years	1971	1976	1981	1986	1991	1996	2001	2006
Population	55.9	56.2	56.4	56.7	57.4	58.2	59.1	60.6

a In which five year interval was the percentage increase the greatest?

b Use the data to estimate what the population will be in the following years.

i 2011 **ii** 2016 **iii** 2021 **iv** 2026 **v** 2031

4 Assess

1 **a** What percentage of this shape is shaded?

b What percentage of the shape is not shaded?

c Another shape has 80% shaded.
What fraction of that shape is shaded?

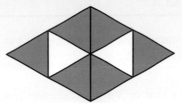

2 Copy and complete the table.
Write each fraction in its simplest form.

Decimal	Fraction	Percentage
0.7		
0.45		
0.625		
	$\frac{1}{4}$	
	$\frac{2}{5}$	
	$\frac{2}{3}$	
		5%
		12.5%
		$33\frac{1}{3}\%$
1.5		
	$2\frac{3}{5}$	
		375%

3 Which of these values are greater than $\frac{1}{2}$?

47%   0.095   8% $\frac{3}{8}$ 0.64

4 Which is the larger amount?
You **must** show your working.

65% of £46 $\frac{3}{5}$ of £52

5 The table shows Carl's marks in two tests.

In which test did Carl do better?
You **must** show your working.

Test	Mark
A	52 out of 80
B	60 out of 100

6 The number of spectators at a football match is 14 594.
3825 of these spectators are season ticket holders.

What percentage are season ticket holders?
Give your answer to the nearest per cent.

7 There are 1246 students in Meera's school. Meera asks
250 of the students what they like to read.

a What percentage of the school population does she ask?

b The table shows her results.

i Why is the total more than 250?

ii What percentage of the students in the survey
like to read magazines?

iii What percentage of the students in the survey
like to read newspapers?

	Number of students
Books	102
Comics	146
Magazines	215
Newspapers	76
Other	85
Total	

D
C

8 The table shows the results of a cycling test.

	Boys	Girls
Pass	34	28
Fail	16	12

Compare the percentage of boys who passed with the percentage of girls who passed.

C

9 The cost of a flight increases from £175 to £210.

Calculate the percentage increase.

10 The population of a village decreases from 2476 to 1947.

Find the percentage decrease in the population.

11 Foollah scored 32 out of 60 in the first maths test.
The second maths test is out of 75.
Overall she needs to score 60% to get a pass in maths.

What mark does she need to score out of 75 in the second test?

	Mark	Maximum
Paper 1	32	60
Paper 2	?	75

12 A farmer has 275 sheep.
80% of the sheep had lambs.
35% of the sheep who had lambs had two lambs.
The rest of the sheep had one lamb.

How many lambs did the sheep have?

13 The table shows Debbie's English and maths test scores in Years 8 and 9.

In which subject has Debbie's test scores improved the most?
You **must** show your working.

	Year 8	Year 9
English	53%	75%
Maths	41%	63%

AQA Examination-style questions

1 **a** The price of a mobile phone is £68.
In a sale the price is decreased by 15%
Work out the price of the mobile phone in the sale.

(3 marks)

   b The number of phones sold increased from 80 to 108.
Work out the percentage increase.

(3 marks)

AQA 2008

Did you know?

A fair world?

Many African countries do not have good healthcare.

In Tanzania, the ratio of doctors to people is 0.02 to 1000. This means one doctor for every fifty thousand people!

People in other countries in the world have better access to a doctor. In Cuba, the ratio is 5.9 to 1000.

In the UK, it is 2.2 to 1000. Think about this next time you are in a surgery waiting room.

You should already know:

✔ how to add, subtract, multiply and divide simple numbers by hand and all numbers with a calculator

✔ how to simplify fractions by hand and by calculator.

Learn... 5.1 Finding and simplifying ratios

Ratios are a good way of comparing quantities such as the number of teachers in a school with the number of students.

The colon symbol is used to express ratio.

In a school with 50 teachers and 800 students, the teacher : student ratio is $50 : 800$

You read $50 : 800$ as '50 to 800'.

Ratios can be simplified like fractions.

Ratio $= 50 : 800$

$\qquad = 5 : 80$ (dividing both numbers by 10)

$\qquad = 1 : 16$ (dividing both numbers by 5)

This is just like simplifying fractions $\dfrac{50}{800} = \dfrac{5}{80} = \dfrac{1}{16}$

Remember that you can use your calculator fraction key to simplify fractions.

The simplest form of the ratio is $1 : 16$. This means there is one teacher for every 16 students, and $\frac{1}{16}$ of a teacher for every student.

The **proportion** of teachers in the school is $\frac{1}{17}$ and the proportion of students is $\frac{16}{17}$

For every 17 people, 1 will be a teacher and 16 will be students. $\frac{1}{17}$ are teachers and $\frac{16}{17}$ are students.

Example: The total price of a meal is £6.16 which includes 66p service charge. What is the ratio of the original meal price to the service charge?

Solution: The original price is £6.16 − £0.66 = £5.50.

So the ratio of original price to service charge is

£5.50 : £0.66 = 550 : 66 (changing both amounts to pence)

$\qquad\qquad\qquad = 50 : 6$ (dividing both numbers by 11)

$\qquad\qquad\qquad = 25 : 3$ (dividing both numbers by 2)

> **AQA Examiner's tip**
>
> A common mistake is to write a ratio with different units. You need to make sure that the units are the same. In this example £5.50 has been changed to pence.

The ratio of the original price to the service charge in its simplest form is $25 : 3$

So for every 25 pence of the original price there is 3 pence of service charge.

For every 25 pence of original price and every 3 pence of service charge there is 28 pence of total charge. The proportion of the total charge that is for service is $\frac{3}{28}$. The proportion of the total charge that is for meal is $\frac{25}{28}$

This means that the original price is $\frac{25}{28}$ of the total price and the service charge is $\frac{3}{28}$ of the total price. Make sure that you understand where these fractions have come from.

Example: A photo is 15 cm high and 25 cm wide. What is the ratio of height to width in its simplest form?

Solution: The ratio of height to width is 15 cm : 25 cm = $15 : 25 = 3 : 5$ (dividing both numbers by 5).

Practise...   5.1 Finding and simplifying ratios 🄺 G F E D C

AQA *Examiner's tip*
Remember that working with ratios is all about
multiplying and dividing not about adding and subtracting.

1 Write each of these ratios as simply as possible.

a	2 : 4	**e**	2 : 12	**i**	24 : 36	**m**	0.3 : 0.8
b	2 : 6	**f**	2 : 14	**j**	25 : 100	**n**	$2\frac{1}{2} . 7\frac{1}{2}$
c	2 : 8	**g**	12 : 36	**k**	$\frac{2}{3} : \frac{4}{9}$	**o**	20% : 80%
d	2 : 10	**h**	18 : 24	**l**	1.5 : 2.5	**p**	25 : 200

2
  a Write down three different pairs of numbers that are in the ratio 1 : 2

  b Explain how you can tell that two numbers are in the ratio 1 : 2

3 Three of these ratios are the same. Which three?

  1 : 2.5   3 : 6   0.2 : 0.5   25 : 55   2 : 5   3 : 7.5

4 Pippa writes the three pairs of numbers 6 and 9, 9 and 12, and 12 and 15.
She says these pairs of numbers are all in the same ratio.
What has Pippa done wrong?

5 A book reading group has men and women in
the ratio 2 : 7

  a There are 21 women in the group.
  How many men are there?

  b Two more men join the group.
  How many more women are needed to keep
  the ratio of men to women the same?

6 On a music download site, a song costs 65p and an album costs £6.50.

  Find the ratio of the cost of a song to the cost of an album in its simplest form.

7 The numbers *a* and *b* are in the ratio 2 : 3

  a If *a* is 4, what is *b*?   **d** If *b* is 1, what is *a*?

  b If *b* is 12, what is *a*?   **e** If *a* and *b* add up to 10, what are *a* and *b*?

  c If *a* is 1, what is *b*?

8 When you enlarge a photograph, the ratio of the
height to width must stay the same. If the ratio is
different the objects in the photograph will look
stretched or squashed.

  a A photo is 20 cm high and 30 cm wide.
  What is the ratio of height to width in its
  simplest form?

  b Another photo measures 25 cm high and 35 cm wide.
  Is the ratio of its width to its height the same as
  the photo in part **a**?

9 A recipe for pastry needs 50 grams of butter and 100 grams of flour.

   a What is the ratio of butter to flour? What is the ratio of flour to butter?

   b How much butter is needed for 200 grams of flour?

   c How much flour is needed for 30 grams of butter?

   d What fraction is the butter's weight of the flour's weight?

10 **a** Find, in their simplest forms, the teacher : student ratios for these schools.

School	Number of teachers	Number of students
School 1	75	1500
School 2	15	240
School 3	22	374
School 4	120	1800
School 5	65	1365

   b **i** A school with 50 teachers has the same teacher : student ratio as School 1. How many students does it have?

      ii If a school with 2000 students had the same teacher : student ratio as School 1. How many teachers does it have?

   c Which school has the smallest number of students for each teacher?

11 Map scales are often expressed in ratio form, such as 1 : 100 000. (This is called a **unitary ratio** as it compares a unit length on the map with the real life length.)

   a Look at some maps (perhaps you can use examples from geography) and write down some examples of how the scales are shown.

   b A scale is written as '2 cm to 1 km'. Write this scale as a unitary ratio.

   c The scale 1 : 100 000 can be written as '1 cm to n km'. Work out the value of n.

   d What distance in real life does 3 cm represent on a 1 : 100 000 map?

Learn... 5.2 Using ratios to find quantities 🄚

You can use ratios to find numbers and amounts.

You can find
- the number of boys and the number of girls in a school

if you know
- the ratio of boys to girls

and
- the total number of students.

For example, in a school of 1000 students, the ratio of boys to girls is 9 : 11

This means that for every 9 boys there are 11 girls, whatever the size of the school.

The total number of parts is 9 + 11 = 20, so

9 out of every 20 students are boys and 11 out of every 20 students are girls.

The fraction of boys in the school is $\frac{9}{20}$ and the fraction of girls in the school is $\frac{11}{20}$

To find the number of boys, work out $\frac{9}{20}$ of 1000.

To find the number of girls, work out $\frac{11}{20}$ of 1000.

$\frac{1}{20}$ of 1000 = 1000 ÷ 20 = 50

Number of boys = 50 × 9 = 450

Number of girls = 50 × 11 = 550

AQA *Examiner's tip*

Check that the number of boys and the number of girls add up to the total number of students in the school.

Example: Jane is 6 years old and Karl is 10 years old.

Their grandmother gives them £24 to share between them in the ratio of their ages.

How much does each child receive?

Solution: The ratio of Jane's age to Karl's age is $6 : 10 = 3 : 5$. (You can use the fraction key on your calculator to simplify the ratio $6 : 10$).

The total number of parts is $3 + 5 = 8$, so Jane gets $\frac{3}{8}$ of £24 and Karl gets $\frac{5}{8}$ of £24.

$\frac{1}{8}$ of £24 is £24 ÷ 8 = £3

So Jane gets $3 \times \frac{1}{8}$ of £24 $= 3 \times £3 = £9$ and Karl gets $5 \times \frac{1}{8}$ of £24 $= 5 \times £3 = £15$.

Practise...   5.2 Using ratios to find quantities 🄺 G F E D C

1   Divide these numbers and quantities in the ratio $1 : 2$

    a   150   **c**   £4.50   **e**   £1.50

    b   300   **d**   6 litres   **f**   1.5 litres

2   Divide the numbers and quantities in Question 1 in the following ratios.

    a $1 : 4$ **c** $3 : 7$

    b $2 : 3$ **d** $1 : 2 : 7$

3   In a savings account, the ratio of the amount invested to the interest paid is $50 : 1$

Approximately how much is the interest paid on a savings account that has £10 525 in it?

4   The angles of any pentagon add up to $540°$.

The angles of one pentagon are in the ratio $2 : 3 : 4 : 5 : 6$

What is the size of the largest angle?

5   This table shows the ratio of carbohydrate to fat to protein in some foods.

Food	Carbohydrate : fat : protein
Chicken sandwich	1 : 1 : 1
Grilled salmon	0 : 1 : 1
Yoghurt (whole milk)	1 : 2 : 1
Taco chips	10 : 4 : 1
Bread	7 : 2 : 1
Milk	2 : 3 : 2

    a   Work out the amount of fat in 150 g of each of the foods.

    b   Which of these foods would you avoid if you were on a low-fat diet?

    c   How many grams of yoghurt would you need to eat to have 100 g of protein?

    d   Which of these foods would you avoid if you were on a low-carbohydrate diet?

D

C

6 Bronze for coins can be made of copper, tin and zinc in the ratio 95 : 4 : 1

   a How much of each metal is needed to make 1 kilogram of bronze?

   b How much of each metal is needed to make 10 kilograms of bronze?

   c How much of each metal is needed to make half a kilogram of bronze?

   d How much zinc would there be in a coin weighing 6 grams?

7 Leena invested £10 000 in a business and Kate invested £3 500.

At the end of the year, Leena and Kate share the profits of £70 000 in the ratio of their investments.

How much does each receive?

8 The table shows the number of pupils in five schools together with the ratio of the number of boys to the number of girls.

School	Total number of students	Boy : girl ratio
School A	750	1 : 1
School B	900	4 : 5
School C	1800	4 : 5
School D	1326	6 : 7
School E	1184	301 : 291

   a Which school contains the greatest number of boys?
   Show working to justify your answer.

   b Which school has the greatest proportion of boys?
   Show working to justify your answer.

Learn... 5.3 Ratio and proportion: the unitary method

The **unitary method** is a very powerful mathematical tool.
The method is based on finding the amount or cost of **one** unit (hence the name 'unitary').

So if you know how much 20 litres of petrol cost, you can find the cost of one litre and then the cost of any number of litres.

20 litres cost £20.60

So 1 litre costs $\frac{£20.60}{20}$ = £1.03 (divide the cost of 20 litres by 20)

Multiply by the cost of 1 litre to find the cost of any number of litres.

You can use the unitary method to do all types of percentages and well as ratio and proportion.

Example: A teacher pays £27.60 for 6 calculators.

How much does he pay for 15 calculators at the same price each?

AQA Examiner's tip

Check your answer is reasonable.

Solution: 6 calculators cost £27.60

So 1 calculator costs $\frac{£27.60}{6}$ = £4.60 (divide the cost of 6 calculators by 6)

So 15 calculators cost 15 × £4.60 (multiply the cost of 1 calculator by 15)

15 × £4.60 = £69

Practise...

5.3 Ratio and proportion: the unitary method

G F E D C

1 Abby travelled for three hours on the motorway and covered 190 miles.

C

a How far would Abby travel in five hours at the same average speed?

b How far would she travel in half an hour?

c How long would it take her to travel 250 miles?

2 Dave drove 246 miles and used 25.4 litres of diesel.

a How many litres of diesel does Dave need for a 400 mile journey?

b How far can he go on 10 litres of diesel?

c What assumptions do you have to make to answer these questions?

3 Here are prices for Minty toothpaste.

Size	Amount of toothpaste	Price
Small	50 ml	£0.99
Standard	75 ml	£1.10
Large	100 ml	£1.28

Which size gives the most toothpaste for one penny?
You **must** show your working.

4 These are prices for different packs of bird seed.

Pack size	Price
5.50 kg	£15.65
12.75 kg	£28.00
25.50 kg	£53.00

a Find the cost of 1 kg of bird seed for each of the different pack sizes.

b Which pack offers best value for money?

c Find the cost of a 25.50 kg pack if the price per kg was the same as for the 5.50 kg pack.

d Give one advantage and one disadvantage of buying a 25.50 kg pack.

! 5 The weights of objects on other planets are proportional to their weights on Earth.
A person weighing 540 newtons on Earth would weigh 90 newtons on the moon and 1350 newtons on Jupiter.

a What would a teenager weighing 360 newtons on Earth weigh on Jupiter?

b What would a rock weighing 10 newtons on the moon weigh on Earth?

c What would an astronaut weighing 130 newtons on the moon weigh on Jupiter?

d Express the ratio 'weight of object on Earth : weight of object on moon : weight of object on Jupiter' in its simplest form.

6 Sajid worked for 8 hours and was paid £30.

a How much will he be paid for working 10 hours at the same rate of pay?

b Complete a copy of this table. Plot the values in the table as points on a graph, using the numbers of hours worked as the *x*-coordinates and the money earned as the corresponding *y*-coordinates.

Number of hours worked	0	2	4	6	8	10
Money earned (£)						

c The points should lie in a straight line through (0, 0).
Explain why the parts should lie on a straight line and pas through (0, 0).

d Show how to use the graph to find out how much Sajid earns in 5 hours.

7 **a** 80% of a number is 16.
What is the number?

b 65% of a number is 195.
What is the number?

8 **a** 90% of a number is 27.
What is the number?

b A sweater is reduced by 10% in a sale. The sale price is £27.
What was the original price?

5 Assess

1 **a** Write each of the following ratios in its simplest form.

   i $6:8$

   ii $27:81$

   iii $1000:10$

   iv $\frac{1}{4}:2$

   v $2\frac{1}{2}:3\frac{1}{2}$

  b **i** In a choir there are 12 boys and 18 girls.
        Express this as a ratio in its simplest form.

   ii Two more boys and two more girls join the choir.
        Express the new ratio in its simplest form.

2 A school has 45 teachers and 810 students. Express the ratio of teachers to students in its simplest form.

3 In a dance class, 30% of the dancers are male. What is the ratio of male dancers to female dancers? Give your answer in its simplest form.

4 To make sugar syrup, 100 grams of sugar is mixed with 250 ml of water.

  a How many grams of sugar are mixed with 1000 ml (one litre) of water?

  b How much water is mixed with 150 grams of sugar?

5 Darren gets 16 out of 20 in Test A and 20 out of 25 in Test B.

  a In which test did he do better?

  b The next test is marked out of 00. How many marks will Darren need in order to do as well as he did on Test A?

6 A litre of paint covers 15 m² of woodwork.

  a How much paint is needed for 50 m² of woodwork?

  b Draw a graph to show the amounts of woodwork covered by amounts of paint up to 6 litres.

7 Divide £12 in the ratio $1:5$

8 Jamie is cooking omelettes.

   To make omelettes for 4 people he uses 6 eggs.

   How many eggs does Jamie need to make omelettes for 10 people?

9 The supermarkets 'Lessprice' and 'Lowerpay' both sell packs of pens.

   'Lessprice' sells a pack of 5 pens for £1.25.

   'Lowerpay' sells a pack of 6 pens for £1.44.

   Which supermarket gives the greater value?

10 It takes Kelly 25 seconds to run 200 m. At the same pace, how long will it take her to run these distances?

   a 56 m

   b 128 m

11 The table shows the approximate population and the number of doctors in some countries of the world.

Country	Population (millions)	Number of doctors
Cuba	10.9	64 300
Israel	5.4	20 600
Italy	57.2	240 000
Nigeria	108.4	30 400
Tanzania	29.7	594
Thailand	58.4	21 600
UK	58.3	128 000
USA	263.6	606 000

   a In which country is the ratio of doctors : population the greatest?

   b Work out the number of doctors in each country if the doctors are shared out equally among the total population.

12 Tom has a total of 100 5p and 10p coins in the ratio 1 : 4

   Jess has a total of 70 10p and 20p coins in the ratio 5 : 2

   Who has the most money?

   You **must** show your working.

AQA Examination-style questions

1 Year 10 and Year 11 students are in an assembly.
Here are some facts about the students in the assembly.

Year	Boys : Girls	Student data
10	4 : 5	84 boys
11	2 : 3	150 students

Work out the total number of girls in the assembly.
You **must** show your working.

(5 marks)

AQA 2008

Objectives

Examiners would normally expect students who get these grades to be able to:

G

find the mode for a set of numbers

find the median for an odd set of numbers

F

work out the range for a set of numbers

calculate the mean for a set of numbers

find the median for an even set of numbers

E

calculate the 'fx' column for a frequency distribution

compare the mean and range of two distributions

D

calculate the mean for a frequency distribution

find the modal class for grouped data

C

find the mean for grouped data

find the median class for grouped data.

Did you know?

The **average** student will:

- sleep for 7 hours per day during the week but 11 hours during the weekend

- spend two and a half hours on the internet after 6 pm on a weekday

- eat 1.7 burgers each week.

Averages

Facts like these can be interesting, but averages are useful in real life. For example, manufacturers need to know how many items to make. They could use data on sales from one month, but this is unlikely to be very reliable. Sales vary from one month to the next, so it's better to take an average over a longer period. Governments also use averages, so they can plan how many houses or hospitals will be needed in future. And if you want to avoid getting into debt it's a good idea to compare your average spending with your average income!

Key terms

average	grouped data
mean	discrete data
median	continuous data
mode	modal class
range	modal group
frequency table	class interval

You should already know:

✔ how to use a calculator to work with the four rules of arithmetic.

Learn... 6.1 Basic measures (k!)

There are three basic measures of **average**.

Mean: To calculate the mean add up all the values and divide this total by the number of values.

Median: To find the median put the numbers in order and find the middle number.

(If there are two numbers in the middle, the median is the mean of these two numbers.)

Mode: To find the mode work out the number (or numbers) which occur most often.

There is one basic measure of spread.

Range: Take away the lowest value from the highest value.

> **AQA** *Examiner's tip*
>
> Students often confuse the different types of average. You must learn which is which and not mix them up.

> **AQA** *Examiner's tip*
>
> Data sets are usually compared using a measure of average and a measure of speed. If you are simply asked to compare two sets of data you have to work these out first.

Example: For this set of data find:

| 3 | 5 | 1 | 2 | 6 | 3 | 6 | 6 |

a the mode   **b** the mean   **c** the median   **d** the range.

Solution:

a mode:

To find the mode work out the number (or numbers) which occur most often.

The number 6 occurs more than any other number, so the mode is 6.

b mean:

To calculate the mean add up all the values and divide the total by the number of values.

Add up all the values $3 + 5 + 1 + 2 + 6 + 3 + 6 + 6 = 32$

Divide this total by the number of values $32 \div 8 = 4$ so the mean $= 4$

c median:

To find the median put the numbers in order and find the middle number.

Put the numbers in order   1   2   3   3   5   6   6   6

Find the middle number   The middle number is the mean of 3 and 5

This is $\frac{3+5}{2} = 4$ so the median $= 4$

d range:

The highest value is 6. The lowest value is 1.

The range is the highest value minus the lowest value.

$6 - 1 = 5$ so the range $= 5$

> **AQA** *Examiner's tip*
>
> Notice how ordering the data helps with the range as well as the median.

Practise... 6.1 Basic measures (k!)

G F E D C

1 For the following sets of data, work out:

a the median

b the mode

c the mean

d the range.

i 4   6   14   5   1

ii 16   19   14   15   15   11

iii 7   5   7   5   7   5   4   8

2 Find the mode, median, mean and range for each of these situations.

a A dice is rolled eleven times and these scores are recorded.

5   1   4   1   1   4   2   3   2   6   4

b A group of twelve fathers were asked how many children they had.

3   1   4   3   1   2   1   1   1   3   2   1

c A local football team plays ten matches and lets in these numbers of goals.

1   0   2   4   0   3   2   1   4   1

d A shopkeeper keeps a record of the number of broken eggs found in eight deliveries.

5   1   5   1   2   0   5   2

3 Josh buys some toffees that cost 62p.

Nicola buys some mints that cost 48p.

Shelley buys some gums that cost 70p.

They share the sweets and share the cost of buying them.

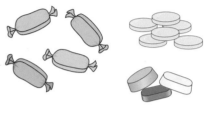

a How much do they pay each?

b What is the name of the average you have calculated?

4 The mean of four numbers is 10.

Three of the numbers are 8, 9 and 10.

Find the fourth number.

5 The median of five numbers is 25.

Four of the numbers are 34, 25, 28 and 17.

Write down a possible value for the fifth number.

6 The mode of five numbers is 8.

Three of the numbers are 6, 7 and 8.

The remaining two numbers are different to each other.

Write down a possible pair of values for the other two numbers.

7 Zoë was having a good year scoring goals in the hockey team.

After 10 matches she had scored: 1, 2, 2, 2, 0, 4, 3, 3, 1, 2 goals.

She said 'A mean of 2 goals is not bad.'

Is Zoë correct? You **must** show your working.

8 Mr Booth, the maths teacher, decided to give his class a test each day for two weeks.

a Teddy's results were 1, 2, 4, 5, 5, 9, 6, 6, 8, 1
Calculate the mean and range of his marks.

b Jasmin's results were 4, 4, 7, 5, 5, 7, 6, 4, 3, 5
Calculate the mean and range of her marks.

c Compare the results of the two students.

9 Ivor is investigating whether teachers or lawyers are more intelligent.

Ivor uses a sample of teachers and a sample of lawyers.

He gives them all the same IQ test.

These are the data for the teachers.

124 116 108 122 117 118 120 131 103 125

These are the data for the lawyers.

121 100 118 129 112 103 102 110 105 119

Give a conclusion about Ivor's investigation.

You must show your working to justify your answer.

10 Write down a set of five numbers with all these features.

The mean is 10.   The median is 9.   The mode is 8.

11 The total of a set of numbers is 100.

The mode is 10.   The range is 5.

Write down a possible set of numbers which meet these conditions.

12 Look at this lift sign.

What does this suggest about the average weight of a person?

The average weight of a group of people in the lift is 90 kg.

> MAXIMUM LOAD
> **8 PERSONS**
> **700 kg**

What is the maximum number of people that can be in the lift without it being overloaded?

Learn... 6.2 Frequency distributions 🎴

A frequency distribution shows how often individual values occur (the frequency).

The information is usually shown in a frequency table.

A **frequency table** shows the values and their frequency.

The frequency table shows the number of pets for students at a school.

Number of pets (x)	Frequency (f)
0	5
1	11
2	8
3	5
4	2

There are 5 students with no pets, 11 students with one pet, 8 students with 2 pets, … and so on.

You can use the frequency table to calculate measures of average and measures of spread.

The **mean** is the total of all the values divided by the number of values. In a frequency table you need to use the formula:

$$\text{Mean} = \frac{\text{the total of (frequencies} \times \text{values)}}{\text{the total of frequencies}} = \frac{\Sigma fx}{\Sigma f} \quad \text{where } \Sigma \text{ means the sum of}$$

The **mode** is the value which has the highest frequency (i.e. the value occurring most often).

The **median** is the middle value when the data are listed in order. It does not matter whether you go from smallest to highest or the other way round.

The **range** is the highest value minus the lowest value.

Example: 🎴 For the frequency distribution above, find:

  a the mean, mode and median

  b the range.

AQA *Examiner's tip*

The average and the spread are useful measures to compare sets of data. You need to understand the difference between measures of average and measures of spread.

Solution: **a**   The mean is the total number of pets divided by the total number of students.

Number of pets (x)	Frequency (f)	Frequency × number of pets (fx)
0	5	$0 \times 5 = 0$
1	11	$1 \times 11 = 11$
2	8	$2 \times 8 = 16$
3	5	$3 \times 5 = 15$
4	2	$4 \times 2 = 8$
	$\Sigma f = 5 + 11 + 8 + 5 + 2 = 31$	$\Sigma fx = 0 + 11 + 16 + 15 + 8 = 50$

$$\text{Mean} = \frac{\text{the total of (frequencies} \times \text{values)}}{\text{the total of frequencies}}$$

$$= \frac{\Sigma fx}{\Sigma f} \quad \text{where } \Sigma \text{ means 'the sum of'}$$

$$= \frac{50}{31}$$

$$= 1.6129$$

Mean = 1.6 (to 1 decimal place)

The mean is a useful measure of average.

> **AQA   Examiner's tip**
>
> Always check that your answers are reasonable. Candidates often mistakenly divide by the number of rows instead of the total frequency. This will usually give a silly answer.

Mode

The mode is the number that occurs most frequently.

1 pet has a frequency of 11 and all the other frequencies are less than this.

Mode = 1

> **AQA   Examiner's tip**
>
> When asked for the mode, make sure that you write down the value (in this case 1), not the frequency (in this case 11).

Median

The median is the middle value when the data are arranged in order.

The data have 31 values so the median is the $\frac{(31 + 1)}{2}$th value = 16th value. The data are already ordered in the table.

The first 5 values are 0, the next 11 are 1, so the 16th value is 1

0 0 0 0 0 1 1 1 1 1 1 1 1 1 1 1 2 2 2 ...

16th

Median = 1

The median can also be found using the 'running totals' of the frequencies as follows:

Number of pets (x)	Frequency (f)	Running total
0	5	5
1	11	$5 + 11 = 16$
2	8	$5 + 11 + 8 = 24$
3	5	$5 + 11 + 8 + 5 = 29$
4	2	$5 + 11 + 8 + 5 + 2 = 31$

The 16th value will lie in this interval so the median is 1.

The range is the highest value minus the lowest value.

b   The range = $4 - 0 = 4$

Range = 4

The range is a measure of how spread out the data are.

> **AQA   Examiner's tip**
>
> Remember that the range should always be presented as a single answer (not a range!).

Practise... 6.2 Frequency distributions 🄚

G F E D C

1 A dice is thrown 100 times. The frequency distribution table shows the scores.

Score (x)	Frequency (f)	Score × frequency (fx)
1	18	
2	19	
3	16	
4	12	
5	15	
6	20	

> **AQA Examiner's tip**
>
> It is possible to use a calculator's statistical functions to find the mean of a frequency distribution. Make sure you are in statistical mode and enter the data value or midpoint followed by its frequency each time.

a Find the mean score.

b Find the median score.

c What is the modal score?

d Work out the range of scores from these 100 dice throws.

e What fraction of the throws resulted in a 6?
Give your answer in its simplest form.

2 The frequency table shows the speed limit of all the roads in one county.

Speed limit (mph)	Number of roads
20	8
30	88
40	52
50	23
60	150
70	3

a How many roads have a speed limit of less than 40 miles per hour?

b What percentage of roads have a 30 miles per hour speed limit?
Give your answer to two decimal places.

c What is the range of speed limits in this county?

d For the data in the frequency table, work out:

   i the modal speed limit

   ii the median speed limit

   iii the mean speed limit.

3 Andy keeps a record of his scores in tennis games.

The table shows results for 40 games he lost.

For the data work out:

a the mean

b the median

c the mode

d the range

e the percentage of games where Andy scored 30 points.

Score	Frequency
0	5
15	8
30	20
40	7

4 The number of people in a sample of 100 cars is given in the frequency table.

Number of people	Frequency
1	60
2	32
3	6
4	2

a Write down the median number of people in these cars.

b Work out the mean number of people in these cars.

c Which is more useful in predicting the number of people in the next car to come along?
Explain your answer.

5 Fill in the frequencies so that the median is 10 and the mode is 9.

x	f
8	
9	
10	
11	

6

x	f
2	34
4	66
6	10
8	*

a If the mode is 8, give a possible value for *. Explain your choice.

b If the median is 4, give a possible value for *. Explain your choice.

7 The table shows the number of bedrooms in a sample of houses from a town centre and a village.

Number of bedrooms	Number of houses	
	Town centre	Village
1	8	3
2	19	9
3	6	10
4	2	8
5	0	5

Hint

As well as using measures of average and spread to make the comparisons you could also use percentages.

Compare the number of bedrooms in these two samples.

8 Two bus companies, Super Express and Big Bus, run a bus service between the same two towns along the same route.

George is investigating the punctuality of their buses on this route.

He records the number of minutes late, rounded to the nearest 5 minutes, for a sample of buses from each company over a one week period.

Here are the data George collects for Big Bus.

0	0	0	0	0	0	0	0	0	0
0	0	0	0	0	0	0	0	5	5
5	5	5	5	5	5	10	10	10	10
10	10	10	10	10	10	15	15	25	35

Here are the data George collects for Super Express.

0	0	0	0	5	5	5	5	5	5
5	5	5	5	5	5	5	5	5	5
5	5	5	10	10	15	15	15	15	15
15	15	15	15	15	15	15	15	15	15
15	20	20	20	20	20	20	20	20	20

Hint

When you are given sets of raw data, the first thing to do is sort out the data in a frequency table.

a Compare the punctuality of the two bus companies.

b Give a reason why you might be more interested in the range of the times late rather than the average.

Learn... 6.3 Grouped frequency distributions

A grouped frequency distribution shows how often **grouped data** values occur (the frequency).

A grouped frequency table shows the values and their frequency.

Grouped frequency distributions are usually used with **continuous data**.

Continuous data are data which can take any numerical value. Length and weight are common examples of continuous data.

Discrete data can only take individual values. Shoe sizes are an example.

You can use the grouped frequency table to calculate measures of average and measures of spread as before.

Mean

The mean is the total of all the values divided by the number of values.

$$\text{Mean} = \frac{\text{the total of (frequencies} \times \text{values})}{\text{the total of frequencies}} = \frac{\Sigma fx}{\Sigma f} \quad \text{where } \Sigma \text{ means 'the sum of'}$$

As the data are grouped, you will need to use the midpoint of each group to represent the value.

Discrete data	Continuous data
To find the midpoint, add together the largest and smallest value of each group and divide the answer by two.	To find the midpoint, add together the smallest possible value (lower bound) and the largest possible value (upper bound) for each group and divide the answer by two.

Bump up your grade

You need to be able to find the mean of grouped data to get a grade C.

Mode

The mode is the value which has the highest frequency next to it (i.e. the value occurring most often).

For grouped data it is more usual to find the modal class.

The **modal class** (or **modal group**) is the class (group) with the highest frequency.

Median

The median is the middle value when the data are listed in order.

For grouped data it is more usual to find the group containing the median.

Graphical work (see Chapter 7) is often used to find the median.

Range

The range is the difference between the highest value minus the lowest value.

For grouped data it is not always possible to identify the highest value and the lowest value. However, it can be estimated as:

Highest value in highest group − lowest value in lowest group.

Example: The table shows the time taken for students to solve a simple puzzle.

$20 \le x < 30$ covers all the values between 20 and 30 seconds. The 20 is included in the group whereas the 30 will be in the $30 \le x < 40$ group.

The range of values within a group is called a **class interval**.

Time in seconds (x)	Frequency
$10 \le x < 20$	30
$20 \le x < 30$	35
$30 \le x < 40$	20
$40 \le x < 50$	10
$50 \le x < 60$	5

Use the information in the grouped frequency table to:

a   write down the modal class

b   work out the class which contains the median

c   calculate an estimate of the mean time taken to solve the puzzle.

Solution:

a The **modal class** is the class with the highest frequency.

This is the class $20 \leqslant x < 30$ (as there are 35 students in this group).

b The median is the middle value when the data are listed in order. In this case the middle value is the 50th value.

The median can be found using the 'running totals' of the frequencies as follows.

The 50th value will lie in this interval so the median lies in the $20 \leqslant x < 30$ class.

Time in seconds (x)	Frequency	Running total
$10 \leqslant x < 20$	30	30
$20 \leqslant x < 30$	35	$30 + 35 = 65$
$30 \leqslant x < 40$	20	$30 + 35 + 20 = 85$
$40 < x < 50$	10	$30 + 35 + 20 + 10 = 95$
$50 \leqslant x < 60$	5	$30 + 35 + 20 + 10 + 5 = 100$

The $20 \leqslant x < 30$ class contains the median.

c As the data are grouped, you need to use the midpoint of each group.

An additional column should be added to the table for the midpoints.

Time in seconds	Frequency (f)	Midpoint (x)	Frequency × midpoint (fx)
$10 \leqslant x < 20$	30	15	$30 \times 15 = 450$
$20 \leqslant x < 30$	35	25	$35 \times 25 = 875$
$30 \leqslant x < 40$	20	35	$20 \times 35 = 700$
$40 \leqslant x < 50$	10	45	$10 \times 45 = 450$
$50 \leqslant x < 60$	5	55	$5 \times 55 = 275$
	$\Sigma f = 100$		$\Sigma fx = 2750$

$$\text{Mean} = \frac{\text{the total of (frequencies} \times \text{values)}}{\text{the total of frequencies}} = \frac{\Sigma fx}{\Sigma f} = \frac{2750}{100} = 27.5$$

Mean = 27.5

Remember that this is only an estimate of the mean as we do not know how the numbers are distributed within each group. Using the midpoint gives an approximation only.

AQA *Examiner's tip*

Remember to check that the answer you have obtained is sensible for the data. Your answer must lie within the range of the data. If it doesn't you have made a mistake.

Practise... 6.3 Grouped frequency distributions 🔑 G F E D C

1 The table shows how long people have to wait to be served in a restaurant.

Time, t (minutes)	Frequency
$0 \leqslant t < 2$	8
$2 \leqslant t < 4$	14
$4 \leqslant t < 6$	6
$6 \leqslant t < 8$	4
$8 \leqslant t < 10$	2

a Write down the modal class.

b In which group does the median lie?

c What percentage of people waited more than 8 minutes? Give your answer to one significant figure.

d Calculate an estimate of the mean waiting time. Explain why your answer is an estimate.

e Estimate the range of the waiting times.

D
C

2 The table shows the weekly wages of 40 staff in a small company.

a Work out:

  i the modal class

  ii the class that contains the median

  iii an estimate of the mean.

b Which average should you use to compare the wages with another company?
Give a reason for your answer.

Wages (£)	Frequency
$50 \leqslant x < 100$	5
$100 \leqslant x < 150$	13
$150 \leqslant x < 200$	11
$200 \leqslant x < 250$	9
$250 \leqslant x < 300$	0
$300 \leqslant x < 350$	2

C

3 The table shows test scores out of 50 for a class of 25 students.

Score	1–10	11–20	21–30	31–40	41–50
Number of students	2	3	12	6	2

Calculate an estimate of the mean weight of a score.

Hint

Apply the rule for discrete data in Learn 6.3.

4 A company produces three million packets of crisps each day.
It states on each packet that the bag contains 25 grams of crisps.
To test this, the crisps in a sample of 1000 bags are weighed.

The table shows the results.

Is the company justified in stating that each bag contains 25 grams of crisps?

You must show your working to justify your answer.

Weight, w (grams)	Frequency
$23.5 \leqslant t < 24.5$	20
$24.5 \leqslant t < 25.5$	733
$25.5 \leqslant t < 26.5$	194
$26.5 \leqslant t < 27.5$	53

Hint

To justify your answer you could:

1. Calculate an estimate of the mean weight of the crisps.

2. Estimate the percentage of packets that contain less than 25 grams.

! 5 Two machines are each designed to produce paper 0.3 mm thick. The tables below show the actual output of a sample from each machine.

	Machine A	Machine B
Thickness, t (mm)	Frequency	Frequency
$0.27 \leqslant t < 0.28$	2	1
$0.28 \leqslant t < 0.29$	7	50
$0.29 \leqslant t < 0.30$	32	42
$0.30 \leqslant t < 0.31$	50	5
$0.31 \leqslant t < 0.32$	9	2

Compare the output of the two machines using suitable calculations.

Which machine is producing paper closer to the required thickness?

6 A school has an attendance target of 95%.
Here are the percentage attendances of students in Class 7A and Class 7B.

Hint

Sort out the data into grouped frequencies before you start.

Class 7A

34	36	48	60	65	78	80	84	84	84
86	88	90	92	94	94	95	95	95	95
95	96	96	96	98	100	100	100	100	

Class 7B

42	42	46	48	48	52	64	68	76	80
86	86	94	94	94	94	94	94	94	94
94	94	96	96	96	98	98	100	100	100

Compare the attendance of each of these classes with the school target.

6 Assess

1   Find the mode, median, mean and range of the following sets of data.

   a   4, 4, 2, 2, 2, 7, 7, 7, 1, 8, 7, 3, 3, 6

   b   3, −3, −3, 2, −2, 1, −1, −1, 0, 0, 1, −1, 2, −1, −2, 3

2   Mr Patel records the marks of 10 students in his record book.

   28,   27,   32,   17,   23,   28,   29,   20,   27,   29

   a   Calculate:

   i   the mean mark   **iii**   the modal mark

   ii   the median mark   **iv**   the range.

   b   He realises that the mark recorded as 32 should have been 35.

   What effect will this have on the following?

   i   the mean mark   **iii**   the modal mark

   ii   the median mark   **iv**   the range.

3   A chart in the Health Centre shows that the average weight of a 6-month-old baby is 7.5 kg. There are six 6-month-old babies at the Health Centre. Their weights are:

   Aneeta 7 kg   Sarah 8 kg   Chris 6.5 kg

   Shivi 7.5 kg   Natalie 6 kg   Sam 8.5 kg

   a   What is the range of the babies' weights?

   b   What is the median weight?

   c   How many babies are over 7.5 kg?

   d   What is the mean weight of the six babies?

   e   Does this group of babies seem to share a similar average weight to those on the chart?
   Explain your answer.

4   The mean of three numbers is 21. Two numbers are smaller than the mean and one is bigger. Write down three possible numbers.

5   In a diving competition, Tom scores a mean mark of 5.3

   Seven of his eight marks are 4.9, 5.3, 5.5, 5.6, 5.8, 4.8, 4.9

   What is his eighth mark?

6   In a survey on the number of people in a household the information shown in the table was collected from 50 houses.

   a   Find the mean, median and mode of household sizes.

   b   Which average is the best one to use to represent the data?
   Explain your answer.

Number of people in a household	Number of households
1	9
2	19
3	9
4	8
5	4
6	1
Total	50

G
F

F
E

E

D

D
C

7 This table gives the number of years service by 50 teachers at the Clare School.

a Find the modal class.

b Calculate an estimate of the mean.

Number of years service	Number of teachers
0–4	11
5–9	15
10–14	4
15–19	10
20–24	6
25–29	4

8 In a science lesson 30 runner bean plants were measured. Here are the results correct to the nearest centimetre.

6.2	5.4	8.9	12.1	6.5	9.3	7.2	12.7	10.2	5.4
7.7	9.5	11.1	8.6	7.0	13.5	12.7	5.6	15.4	12.3
13.4	9.5	6.7	8.6	9.1	11.5	14.2	13.5	8.8	9.7

The teacher suggested putting the data into groups.

Length in centimetres	Tally	Total
5 but less than 7		
7 but less than 9		
9 but less than 11		
11 but less than 13		
13 but less than 15		
15 but less than 17		

a Copy and complete the table.

b Use the information to estimate the mean height of the plants.

c Calculate the mean from the original data.

d Why is your answer to part **b** only an estimate of the mean?

9 The weights of some apples are shown in the table.

Weight of apples, w grams	Frequency
$30 < w \leqslant 40$	25
$40 < w \leqslant 50$	28
$50 < w \leqslant 60$	21
$60 < w \leqslant 70$	6

Granny Smith apples have a mean weight of 45 grams and a range of 39 grams.

Compare these data with the table. Do the data in the table seem to be about Granny Smith apples?

AQA Examination-style questions

1 a Here are four numbers.

4   2   1   7

Explain why the median is 3. *(2 marks)*

b Here are five numbers.

4   2   1   7   5

What fraction of the numbers is below the median? *(2 marks)*

c A set of six numbers has a median of 3. Only one of the numbers is below the median.

Write down a possible set of the six numbers. *(2 marks)*

AQA 2008

Objectives

Examiners would normally expect students who get these grades to be able to:

G

construct and interpret a pictogram

construct and interpret a bar chart

F

construct and interpret a dual bar chart

interpret a pie chart

E

construct a pie chart

interpret a stem-and-leaf diagram

D

construct a stem-and-leaf diagram (ordered)

construct a histogram for data with equal class intervals

interpret a line graph

C

construct a frequency polygon.

Key terms

pictogram
bar chart
pie chart
key
dual bar chart
composite bar chart
stem-and-leaf diagram

back-to-back stem-and-leaf diagram
line graph
frequency polygon
frequency diagram
histogram

Did you know?

A. Favourite pies

B. Favourite pies

apple
pork
steak
chicken

Favourite pie chart!

Charts and diagrams can sometimes be misleading. Look at the two pie charts above.

Which is the most popular pie shown in Chart A?

Which is the most popular pie shown in Chart B?

Is chicken pie more popular in Chart A or Chart B?

Without knowing the underlying data, it can be difficult to interpret the charts.

In fact, each of the two charts represents exactly the same set of data.

Apple pie is the favourite pie.

The proportions only look different because of the way the pie charts have been drawn.

3-D charts can misrepresent data.

Beware when representing data. Not every picture tells the same story!

You should already know:

✔ the measures of average: mean, mode and median

✔ how to find and work with the range

✔ how to measure and draw angles

✔ types of data, e.g. discrete and continuous, qualitative and quantitative

✔ the meaning of inequality signs

✔ how to construct and interpret a tally chart

✔ how to work with percentages and fractions.

Learn... 7.1 Pictograms, bar charts and pie charts

Pictograms, **bar charts** and **pie charts** are used to display either qualitative data or discrete quantitative data.

Qualitative data involve a description or feature, and are not numerical (a quality).

Quantitative data involve numbers of some kind (a quantity).

Link

Remind yourself about different types of data by looking at Chapter 3.

Pictograms

A symbol is used to represent a certain number of items.

A **key** shows the number of items each symbol stands for.

For example: Key: 🍦 = 2 ice creams.

You can use part symbols for fewer items.

For example, 🍦 = 1 ice cream.

AQA Examiner's tip

Remember to draw symbols the same size and line them up.

The diagram should also be given a title.

Example: Here are some data on the top favourite crisp flavours for a class of students in Year 10.

Flavour	Salt and vinegar	Cheese and onion	Ready salted
Number of students (frequency)	6	7	10

Draw a pictogram to show these data.

Solution: First you must decide on a symbol and how many it will represent. As the data only go up to 10, a symbol representing 2 students will be fine.

Often you can use a symbol connected to the situation.

AQA Examiner's tip

You may be asked to draw a pictogram in the exam. You will save time if your symbol represents more than one item.

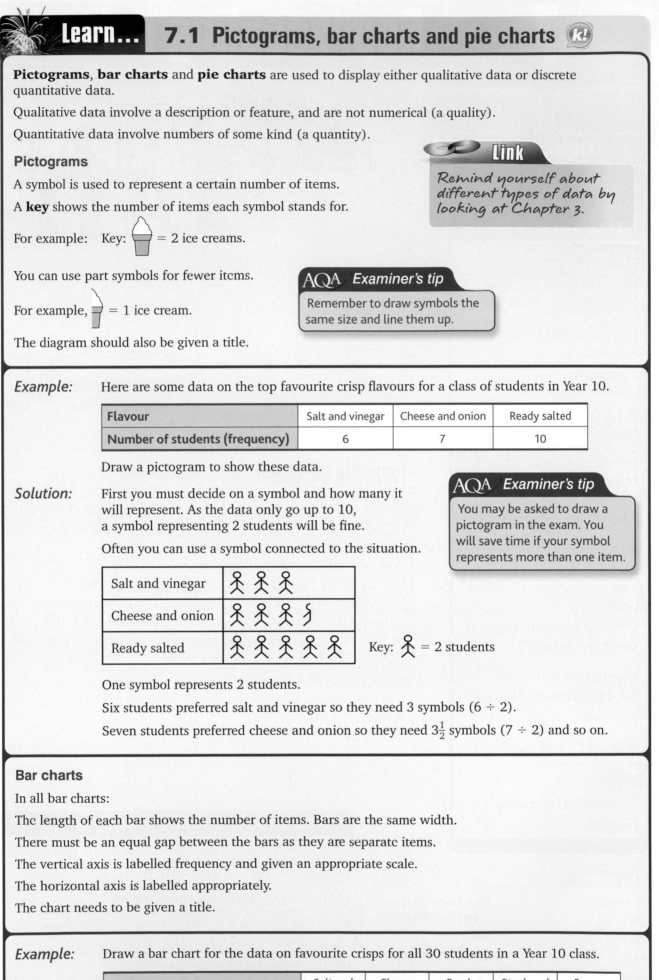

Salt and vinegar	🧍 🧍 🧍
Cheese and onion	🧍 🧍 🧍 🧍
Ready salted	🧍 🧍 🧍 🧍 🧍

Key: 🧍 = 2 students

One symbol represents 2 students.

Six students preferred salt and vinegar so they need 3 symbols (6 ÷ 2).

Seven students preferred cheese and onion so they need $3\frac{1}{2}$ symbols (7 ÷ 2) and so on.

Bar charts

In all bar charts:

The length of each bar shows the number of items. Bars are the same width.

There must be an equal gap between the bars as they are separate items.

The vertical axis is labelled frequency and given an appropriate scale.

The horizontal axis is labelled appropriately.

The chart needs to be given a title.

Example: Draw a bar chart for the data on favourite crisps for all 30 students in a Year 10 class.

Flavour	Salt and vinegar	Cheese and onion	Ready salted	Steak and onion	Prawn cocktail
Number of students (frequency)	6	7	10	5	2

Solution:

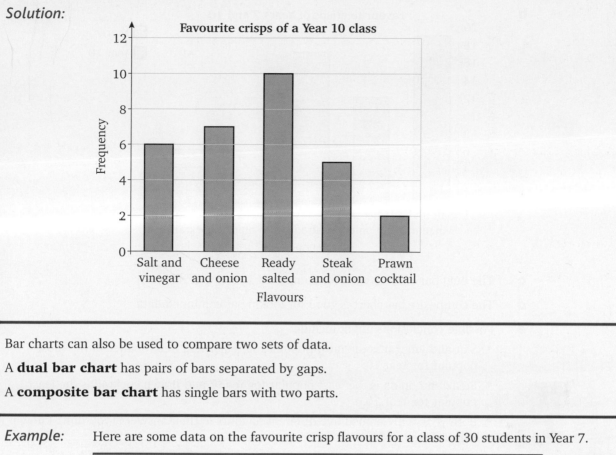

Bar charts can also be used to compare two sets of data.

A **dual bar chart** has pairs of bars separated by gaps.

A **composite bar chart** has single bars with two parts.

Example: Here are some data on the favourite crisp flavours for a class of 30 students in Year 7.

Flavour	Salt and vinegar	Cheese and onion	Ready salted	Steak and onion	Prawn cocktail
Number of students	13	5	7	1	4

a   Draw a dual bar chart to show these data and the data from Year 10 given above.

b   Draw a composite bar chart to show these data.

c   Give one advantage of using the dual bar chart.

d   Give one advantage of using the composite bar chart.

e   Compare the students' favourite crisps. What conclusions do you reach?

Solution: **a**

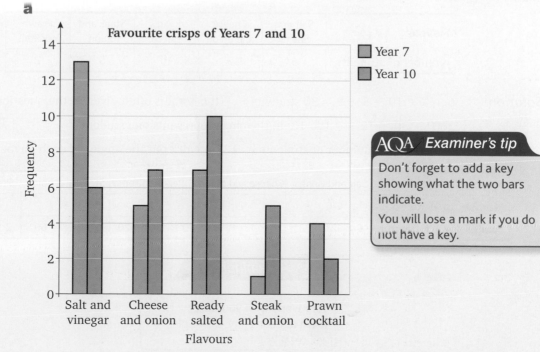

AQA *Examiner's tip*

Don't forget to add a key showing what the two bars indicate.

You will lose a mark if you do not have a key.

b

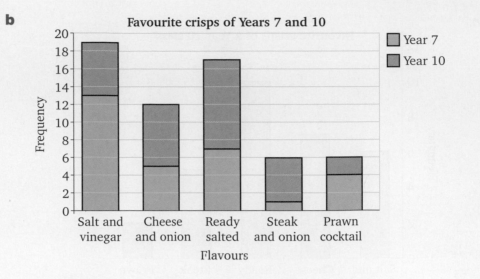

c The dual bar chart is good for comparing two sets of data.

d The composite bar chart is good for looking at combined data.

e Possible conclusions might include:

- Salt and vinegar is the most popular for Year 7 and Ready salted is the most popular for Year 10.
- Steak and onion is the least popular for Year 7 and Prawn cocktail is the least popular for Year 10.
- Both years only named five different flavours in their answers (you don't know if it was a closed question or an open question).

Pie charts

In a pie chart, the frequency is represented by the angle (or area) of a sector of a circle.

Use the fact that the angles in a circle add up to 360°.
Pie charts either need a key or each factor must be labelled.

Don't forget the title.

> **AQA Examiner's tip**
>
> You will lose marks if you do not have a key or forget to label your pie chart.

Example: 📘 Draw a pie chart to show the data for the favourite crisps of Year 10.

Flavour	Salt and vinegar	Cheese and onion	Ready salted	Steak and onion	Prawn cocktail
Number of students	6	7	10	5	2

Solution: 6 + 7 + 10 + 5 + 2 = 30 students   (this total is often given in the question)

360° ÷ 30 = 12°   (So 12° in the circle represents one student)

Multiply each number of students by 12° to work out the angle for each flavour.

Flavour	Salt and vinegar	Cheese and onion	Ready salted	Steak and onion	Prawn cocktail
Number of students	6	7	10	5	2
Angle for each flavour	6 × 12° = 72°	7 × 12° = 84°	10 × 12° = 120°	5 × 12° = 60°	2 × 12° = 24°

> **AQA Examiner's tip**
>
> Add up all the angles to check your working. If you have worked them out correctly, the angles will total 360°.

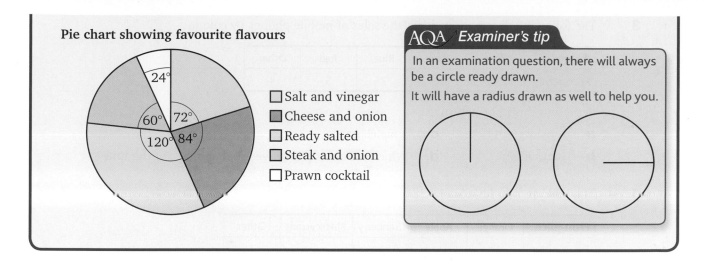

Pie chart showing favourite flavours

24°
60° 72°
120° 84°

☐ Salt and vinegar
◼ Cheese and onion
☐ Ready salted
◼ Steak and onion
☐ Prawn cocktail

AQA Examiner's tip

In an examination question, there will always be a circle ready drawn.
It will have a radius drawn as well to help you.

Practise... 7.1 Pictograms, bar charts and pie charts k! G F E D C

G

1   The pictogram shows the number of cars owned by families in one street.

	Number of families
No cars	🚗 🚗 🚗
One car	🚗 🚗 🚗 🚗 🚗 🚗
Two cars	🚗 🚗 🚗
Three cars	🚗

Key: 🚗 represents 10 families

a   How many families did not own a car?

b   How many families owned two or more cars?

2   The pictogram shows the number of ice creams sold over five days.

Day	Number of ice creams sold
Monday	🍦 🍦 🍦 🍦 🍦
Tuesday	🍦 🍦 🍦 🍦 🍦 🍦 🍦 🍦
Wednesday	
Thursday	🍦 🍦 🍦 🍦
Friday	🍦 🍦 🍦 🍦 🍦 🍦

Key: 🍦 = 4 ice creams

a   How many ice creams were sold on Monday?

b   How many ice creams were sold on Friday?

c   On what day were most ice creams sold?

G D

3   The following distribution shows the sales of mobile phones by colour.

Colour	Silver	Black	Blue	Red	Other
Frequency	14	10	3	5	4

Represent this information as:

a   a pictogram   **c**   a pie chart

b   a bar chart   **d**   Which colour of phone was sold about $\frac{1}{12}$ of the time?

4   The table shows the sales of fruit juices.

Fruit juice	Orange	Apple	Cranberry	Blackcurrant	Other
Frequency	18	8	3	6	1

a   Represent this information as:

    i   a pictogram

    ii   a bar chart

    iii   a pie chart.

b   Which diagram is best for comparing the different fruit juices sold? Give a reason for your answer.

c   Which fruit juice has sales that are just over 20% of the total sales?

F D

5   Ian has to track emails and faxes over one week at the office.

The graph shows a dual bar chart for the number of emails and faxes received on five days of a week.

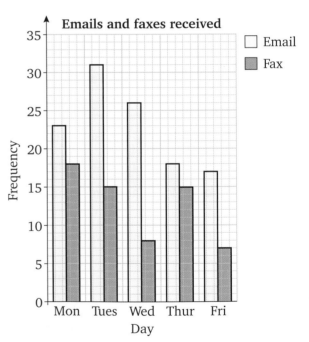

a   Copy and complete the following table for the number of emails and faxes received.

Day	Emails	Faxes
Monday		
Tuesday		
Wednesday		
Thursday		
Friday		

b   What is the modal number of emails?

c   What is the modal number of faxes?

d   Calculate the range for the number of emails.

e   Which day had the least number of faxes?

6   The table shows the gas and electricity bills (in pounds to the nearest pound) for the quarters in one year.

Quarter	Gas	Electricity
1st quarter	85	93
2nd quarter	52	68
3rd quarter	15	47
4th quarter	44	61

a   Show these data in a dual bar chart.

b   Show these data in a composite bar chart.

c   Give one advantage of each of your charts in part **a** and part **b**.

d   What percentage of gas costs for the year are billed in the 1st quarter?

e   Compare the costs of gas and electricity throughout the year.

7   The table shows how 180 students travelled to college.

Travel	Car	Bus	Taxi	Walk	Cycle
Frequency	88	22	7	40	23

Use a suitable diagram to represent these data.

8   Some students are asked to choose their favourite type of film.

Their choices are shown in the pie chart.

A total of 135 students choose horror films.

a   How many students choose thrillers?

Twice as many students choose 'Comedy' as choose 'Romance'.

b   How many students chose 'Comedy'?

c   Carry out a similar survey in your school.
Draw a pie chart of the results and make comparisons
of the results.

Favourite film

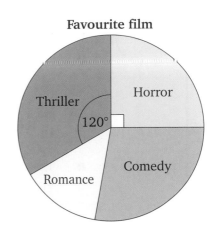

Learn...   7.2 Stem-and-leaf diagrams

Stem-and-leaf diagrams are a useful way of representing data. They are used to show discrete data, or continuous data that have been rounded.
Stem-and-leaf diagrams need a key to show the 'stem' and 'leaf'.

For two-digit numbers the first digit (tens) is the stem and the 2nd digit (units) is the leaf.

Stem (tens)	Leaf (units)
1	6 8 1 9 7
2	7 8 2 7 7 2 9
3	4 1 6

In this case the number 6 stands
for 16 (1 ten and 6 units).

In this case the number 6 stands
for 36 (3 tens and 6 units).

It is often useful to provide **an ordered stem-and-leaf diagram** where the items are placed in order.

Stem (tens)	Leaf (units)
1	1 6 7 8 9
2	2 2 7 7 7 8 9
3	1 4 6

Here the leaves (units) are
arranged numerically.

Key: 3 | 1 represents 31

For three-digit numbers the first digit (hundreds) is often used as the stem and the other digits are the leaves.

For example 5 | 67 might represent 567.

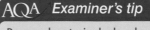 **Hint**

Stem-and-leaf diagrams are useful because
they show all the actual data values in a set
of data. It is the only diagram that does this.

AQA *Examiner's tip*

Remember to include a key for a
stem-and-leaf diagram. If you don't
include a key you will lose marks.

Example: A sample of 25 children in a primary school record how many portions of fruit and vegetables they eat from Monday to Friday.

23	37	14	32	42	38	15	33	27	20	31	19	18
26	25	38	31	32	28	34	25	22	17	12	22	

a   Draw an ordered stem-and-leaf diagram for the data.

b   Work out the range of the results.

c   Work out the median number of portions eaten.

d   The Government advises that you should eat at least five portions of fruit and vegetables a day.

   i   What fraction of children have followed this advice?

   ii   What percentage of children have followed this advice?

   iii   What assumption did you make in answering these questions?

Solution: **a**   The data run from 12 to 42 so the stem will represent the tens.

The stem will be 1, 2, 3 and 4 placed in a vertical line.

The leaves will represent the units.

For example, the first value recorded is 23 so write a 3 alongside the stem value of 2.

You will now have an unordered stem-and-leaf diagram. The diagram is unordered as the leaves are not in order.

> **AQA Examiner's tip**
>
> Always complete an unordered diagram first. It is then far easier to complete the ordered one. There will always be space to do this on the exam paper.

Unordered stem-and-leaf showing portions of fruit and vegetables eaten

Now write the leaves in order to give an ordered stem-and-leaf diagram.

Remember to include a key.

```
1 | 4  5  9  8  7  2
2 | 3  7  0  6  5  8  5  2  2
3 | 7  2  8  3  1  8  1  2  4
4 | 2
```

Ordered stem-and-leaf showing portions of fruit and vegetables eaten

Notice how the diagram looks a little like a bar chart or pictogram in that it is easy to see where most data lie.

```
1 | 2  4  5  7  8  9
2 | 0  2  2  3  5  5  5  6  7  8
3 | 1  1  2  2  3  4  7  8  8
4 | 2
```

Key: 3 | 1 represents 31 portions of fruit and vegetables

b   Range = highest value minus lowest value

$$= 42 - 12$$
$$= 30$$

> **AQA Examiner's tip**
>
> Don't forget to include the stem number in your answer. For example, here you must say that the median is 26, not 6.

c   The median is the middle value when values are put in order.

In an ordered stem-and-leaf diagram the data are in order.

There are 25 values so the median is the $\left(\dfrac{25 + 1}{2}\right)$th value or the 13th value.

Counting along this gives 26 portions.

In 5 days, you should eat $5 \times 5 = 25$ portions.

d   **i**   Looking at the diagrams, 15 out of 25 have eaten 25 or more portions.

Fraction is $\dfrac{15}{25} = \dfrac{3}{5}$

   ii   Percentage is $\dfrac{3}{5} \times 100 = 60\%$

   iii   The number of portions of fruit and vegetables is spread evenly over the days.

Two data sets can be shown at the same time on a **back-to-back stem-and-leaf diagram**.

This example of a back-to-back stem-and-leaf diagram compares the portions of frut eaten by boys and girls. Each side of the diagram then needs a stem label.

7	7	6	5	4	2	2	1	1	6	7	8	9		
	7	6	4	3	2	1	2	2	2	7	7	7	8	9
					7	0	3	1	4	6				

Key: 7 | 1 represents 17   Key: 1 | 7 represents 17

Notice the leaves run from right to left in order of size on the left side of the diagram.

This also means you need a key for **each side** of the diagram.

Practise...   7.2 Stem-and-leaf diagrams   G F E D C

1   The prices paid for a selection of items from a supermarket are as follows.

45p   32p   38p   21p   66p   54p   60p   44p   35p   42p   44p

Show the data in an ordered stem-and-leaf diagram.

D

2   The marks obtained by some students in a test were recorded as follows.

8   20   9   21   18   22   19   13   22   24
14   9   25   10   19   20   17   14   12

a   Show this information in an ordered stem-and-leaf diagram.

b   What was the highest mark in the test?

c   Write down the median of the marks in the test.

d   Write down the range of the marks in the test.

e   The pass mark for the test was 15 marks.
        What fraction of the students passed the test?

3   The times taken to complete an exam paper were recorded as follows.

2 h 12 min,   1 h 53 min,   1 h 26 min,   2 h 26 min,   1 h 50 min,

1 h 46 min,   2 h 05 min,   1 h 43 min,   1 h 49 min,   2 h 10 min,

1 h 49 min,   1 h 55 min,   2 h 06 min,   1 h 57 min.

a   Convert all the times to minutes.

b   Show the converted data in an ordered stem-and-leaf diagram.

C

⚠ 4   A set of 31 pieces of data has the following:

Minimum value of 23

Maximum value of 65

Median of 44

Mode of 42 and 55

Draw a possible stem-and-leaf diagram making up data values which satisfy these conditions.

5   Emma is investigating this hypothesis: Girls take longer to complete an exercise than boys.

She collects the data shown in this back-to-back stem-and-leaf diagram.

Number of minutes to complete a task

Leaf (units) Girls	Stem (tens)	Leaf (units) Boys
7 7 6 5 4 2 2	1	1 6 7 8 9
7 6 4 3 2 1	2	2 2 7 7 7 8 9
7 0	3	1 4 6

Key: 3 | 2 represents 23 minutes   Key: 3 | 4 represents 34 minutes

Write some conclusions that Emma might make about her hypothesis.
You must show your working to justify your answer.

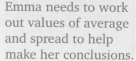

Hint
Emma needs to work out values of average and spread to help make her conclusions.

6   Declan is investigating reaction times for Year 7 and Year 11 students.

In an experiment he obtains these results.

Year	Times (tenths of a second)													
7	18	19	09	28	10	04	11	14	15	18	09	27	28	06	05
11	07	20	09	12	21	17	11	12	15	08	09	12	08	16	19

a   Show this information in a back-to-back stem-and-leaf diagram.

b   Declan thinks Year 7 have quicker reaction times than Year 11.
Use your diagram to show whether he is correct.

7   A village football team played 32 games during one season.

The number of spectators for the first 31 games is shown
in the stem-and-leaf diagram.

a   The number of spectators at the 32nd game
increases the range by 14.
Work out two possible values for the number of
spectators at the 32nd game.

b   Do either of these possible values affect the median of
the number of spectators after 31 games?
Explain your answer.

c   Do either of the possible values found in part **a** affect the modal number of spectators after
31 games.
Explain your answer.

18	4 6
19	0 2 3 5
20	3 3 7 9 9 9 9
21	0 1 5 5 6 7 8 8 9
22	3 4 4 6 9
23	2 5
24	7 8

Key: 18 | 4 represents 184 spectators

Learn...   7.3 Line graphs, frequency polygons and histograms

Line graphs

A **line graph** is a series of points joined with straight lines.

Line graphs show how data change over a period of time.

Example: The table shows the temperature of a patient at different times during the day.

Time	10.00	11.00	12.00	13.00	14.00
Temperature (°F)	102.5	101.3	102	99.1	99.2

Draw a line graph to show this information.

Solution: Plot the points and join them up with straight lines.

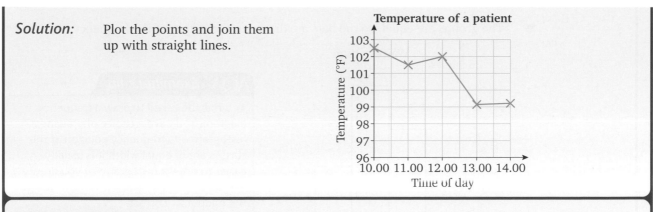

Temperature of a patient

Frequency polygons

A **frequency polygon** is a way of showing continuous grouped data in a diagram.

Points are plotted at the midpoint of each class interval. The groups may have equal or unequal widths.

The frequency polygon is an example of a **frequency diagram**.

Another type of frequency diagram is a **histogram**.

Histograms

A histogram is a way of showing continuous grouped data in a diagram. The area of the bar represents the frequency.

The groups may have equal or unequal widths. At Foundation Tier all histograms will have equal width groups.

Histograms with equal group widths

If the group widths are equal, bars are drawn to the height of the frequency.

Example: 50 people were asked how long they had to wait for a train.
The table below shows the results.

Time, t (minutes)	Frequency
$5 \leqslant t < 10$	16
$10 \leqslant t < 15$	22
$15 \leqslant t < 20$	11
$20 \leqslant t < 25$	1

a Draw a frequency polygon to represent the data.

b Draw a histogram to represent the same data.

> AQA *Examiner's tip*
>
> Make sure that the axes are labelled properly and not in terms of class intervals.

Solution: **a** For a frequency polygon, the points are plotted at the midpoint of each class interval.

E.g. the midpoint for $5 \leqslant t < 10$ is $\dfrac{5 + 10}{2} = 7.5$

Frequency polygon to show waiting times

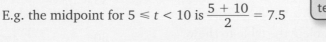

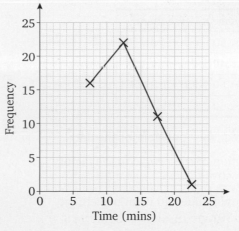

> AQA *Examiner's tip*
>
> There is no need to draw lines beyond the first and last plots.

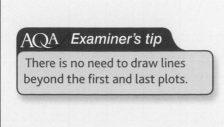

b   The groups are equal, so the bars are drawn to the height of the frequency.

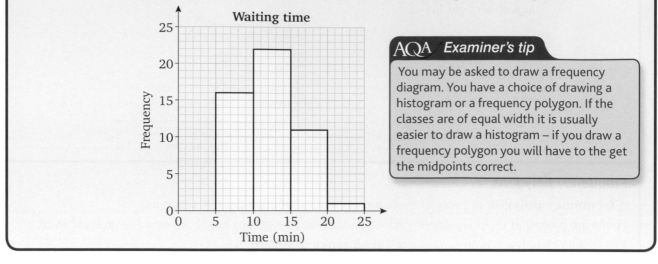

Waiting time

AQA *Examiner's tip*

You may be asked to draw a frequency diagram. You have a choice of drawing a histogram or a frequency polygon. If the classes are of equal width it is usually easier to draw a histogram – if you draw a frequency polygon you will have to the get the midpoints correct.

7.3 Line graphs, frequency polygons and histograms

Practise...

G F E D C

1   The table shows the times of runners in a fun run.

Time, t (minutes)	Frequency
5 up to 10	40
10 up to 15	125
15 up to 20	100
20 up to 25	55
25 up to 30	15

Draw a histogram for the data.

2   The table shows the time spent in a local shop by 60 customers.

a   Draw one type of frequency diagram for the data.

b   Draw a different type of frequency diagram for the data.

Time, t (minutes)	Frequency
$5 \leq t < 10$	8
$10 \leq t < 15$	30
$15 \leq t < 20$	16
$20 \leq t < 25$	6

3   The frequency diagram shows the ages of 81 people in a factory.

a   Copy and complete the table to show this information.

Age, y (years)	Frequency
$20 \leq y < 30$	
$30 \leq y < 40$	
$40 \leq y < 50$	
$50 \leq y < 60$	

b   Draw a frequency polygon for the data.

c   What fraction of the people in the factory are under 40?

d   Of the people under 40 what percentage are under 30?

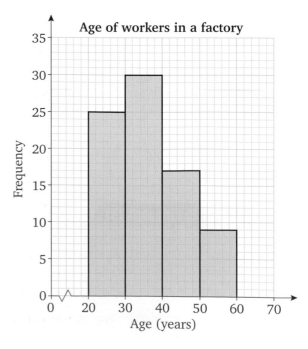

Age of workers in a factory

4 The table shows the pressure in millibars (mb) over five days at a seaside resort.

Day	Pressure (mb)
Monday	1018
Tuesday	1022
Wednesday	1028
Thursday	1023
Friday	1019

a Draw a line graph to show the pressure each day.

b What do you assume when drawing this line graph?

5 The table shows the minimum and maximum temperatures at a seaside resort.

Draw a line graph to show:

a the minimum temperatures

b the maximum temperatures.

Day	Minimum temperature (°C)	Maximum temperature (°C)
Monday	15	19
Tuesday	11	21
Wednesday	13	22
Thursday	14	23
Friday	17	23

Use your graph to find:

c the day on which the lowest temperature was recorded

d the day on which the highest temperature was recorded

e the biggest difference between the daily minimum and maximum temperatures.

f Collect data about minimum and maximum temperatures for different parts of the world over one week. You should find data in most daily newspapers or on the internet.

Draw suitable graphs to compare different places.

6 The head teacher of a college thinks that attendance becomes worse as the week progresses.

The table shows the number of students at college present during morning and afternoon registration.

Day	Mon	Mon	Tue	Tue	Wed	Wed	Thu	Thu	Fri	Fri
Session	am	pm	am	pm	am	pm	am	pm	am	pm
Number	220	210	243	215	254	218	251	201	185	152

a Show this information on a graph.

b There are 260 students in the college.
Work out the percentage attending each registration session.
Give your answers to the nearest whole number.

c Do your answers to parts **a** and **b** support the head teacher?
Explain your answer.

7 The table shows the cost of electricity bills at the end of every three months.

Year	2006	2006	2006	2006	2007	2007	2007	2007
Quarter	1st	2nd	3rd	4th	1st	2nd	3rd	4th
Cost	£230	£120	£50	£80	£215	£120	£25	£55

a Show this information on a graph.

b Describe any patterns in the data.

7

Assess

1 The graph shows the number of people in a library each day at noon.

   a Write down the number of people in the library each day at noon.

   b On which of these days is the library closed at noon?

   c Give two reasons why the graph does **not** show that more people visit on a Saturday than any other day.

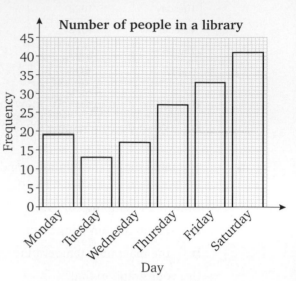

2 The pictogram shows the number of DVDs sold in a shop during Monday morning.

   a What time do you think the shop opens? Give a reason for your answer.

   b How many DVDs were sold between 9 am and 9.30 am?

   c What proportion of the morning sales is made before 10 am?

   d The mean profit on a DVD sold is £2.56. The cost of running the shop is £12.04 per hour. Does the shop make an overall profit on Monday morning?

   You **must** show your working.

Time period	Number of DVDs sold
9.00 – 9.30	◎ ◎
9.30 – 10.00	◖
10.00 – 10.30	◎ ◎ ◎ ◎ ◖
10.30 – 11.00	◎ ◎
11.00 – 11.30	◎
11.30 – 12.00	◎ ◎ ◖

Key: ◎ = 2 DVDs sold

3 The pie charts below show how 200 students travel to college one day during winter and one day during summer.

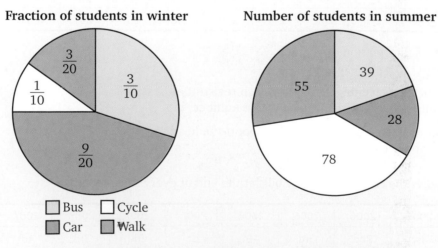

   a Work out the angles for each method of travel for each chart.

   b Compare the methods of travel for the different times of the year.

   c Sandy said 'This proves more people walk to college in summer'. Is Sandy correct? Give a reason for your answer.

4 The heights of the 40 workers in a factory are given in the diagram below.

Females		Males
9	14	
9 8 2	15	
9 9 8 7 6 6 6 4 4 3 1	16	2 4 7 9 9
8 7 5 3 3 2 2 1	17	2 2 4 5 5 8
2	18	3 3 6 9
	19	1

Key: 7 | 16 represents 167 cm   Key: 18 | 3 represents 183 cm

a Explain why the median male height is 174.5 cm.

b Show that only about 19% of males are shorter than the median female height.

c Compare the ranges of the male and female heights.

d Produce a similar diagram for data from your class.

5 For each of these tables of data, draw an appropriate graph.

Table A

Five coins were thrown together 100 times and the number of tails showing uppermost was recorded as shown below.

Number of tails	Frequency
0	2
1	17
2	29
3	34
4	15
5	3

Table B

Four different airlines make the following number of flights from a regional airport.

Airline	Number of flights
Big Wing	12
Fly Maybe	9
Squeezyjet	4
Fly on Air	7

Table C

Vinoj and Ling went fishing every month for six years.

They keep the following record of the number of fish caught each month.

One number needs to be filled in before you can draw a graph.

Number caught	Frequency
$0 \leqslant n \leqslant 10$	3
$10 < n \leqslant 20$	17
$20 < n \leqslant 30$	31
$30 < n \leqslant 40$	19
$40 < n \leqslant 50$	?

D

6 The number of workers in the staff restaurant in a hospital is shown in the line graph.

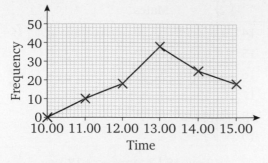

a At what time is the restaurant busiest?

b What time do you think the restaurant opens?
Give a reason for your answer.

c Complete this table.

Time	10.00	11.00	12.00	13.00	14.00	15.00
Number of workers in restaurant						

d Is a line graph a suitable diagram for these data?

e Display the data in a suitable diagram of your choice.

7 Draw a suitable ordered stem-and-leaf diagram for the following data.

The distance travelled by 15 motorists alone and by 15 motorists with passengers.

Distance travelled alone	22	3	12	31	6	10	19	25	9	4	11	16	14	26	8
Distance travelled with passengers	25	10	7	27	37	37	21	48	23	4	13	33	37	25	33

For your diagram, write down three features you notice.

AQA Examination-style questions 🔑

1 The bar chart shows the number of men and women visiting a dentist in one week.
The bar for women on Friday is missing.

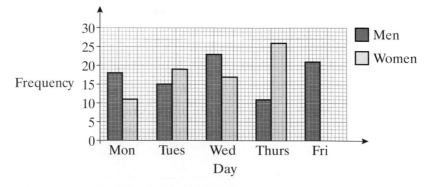

a How many women visited the dentist on Tuesday? *(1 mark)*

b How many men and women in total visited the dentist on Monday? *(2 marks)*

c During that week an equal number of men and women visited the dentist.
How many women visited the dentist on Friday? *(4 marks)*

AQA 2008

Scatter graphs

Did you know?

Scatter graphs

Scatter graphs are frequently used in medical research to test for relationships. For example, a study of office workers found that those with a stressful job had higher blood pressure. Scatter graphs can also be used to test the effects of drugs on lowering blood pressure.

You should already know:

✔ how to use coordinates to plot points on a graph

✔ how to draw graphs including labelling axes and adding a title.

Learn... 8.1 Plotting points on a scatter graph

Scatter graphs (or scatter diagrams) are used to show the relationship between two sets of data.

Before drawing a scatter graph you need to identify the scale on the axes.

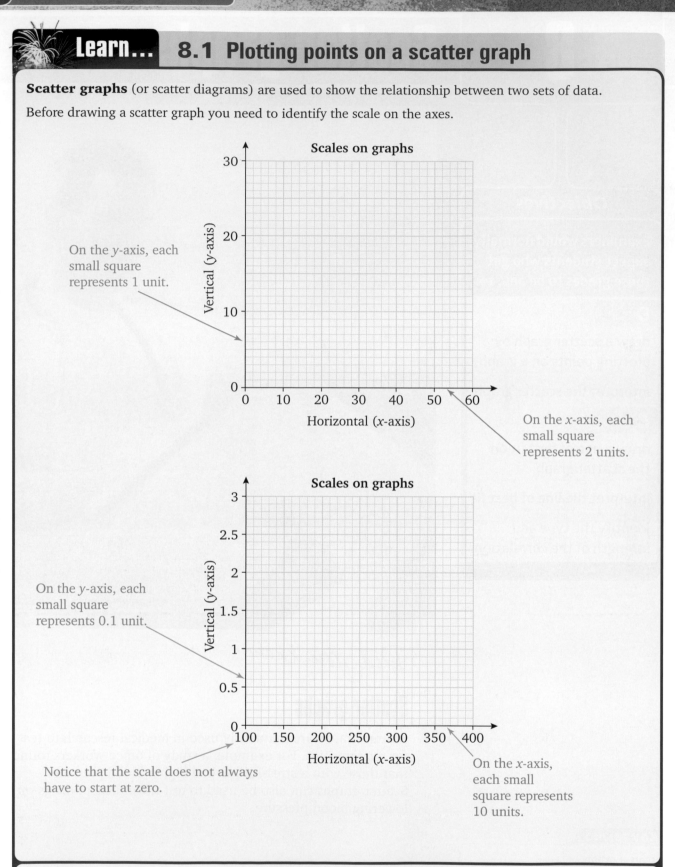

On the *y*-axis, each small square represents 1 unit.

On the *x*-axis, each small square represents 2 units.

On the *y*-axis, each small square represents 0.1 unit.

Notice that the scale does not always have to start at zero.

On the *x*-axis, each small square represents 10 units.

Example: The table shows the temperature and numbers of ice creams sold on different days.

	Sun	Mon	Tue	Wed	Thu	Fri	Sat
Temperature (°C)	20	26	17	24	30	15	18
Ice cream sales	35	39	27	36	45	25	32

Show this information on a scatter graph.

Solution: The information can be plotted on a scatter graph using the **coordinate** points shown.

	Sun	Mon	Tue	Wed	Thu	Fri	Sat
Temperature (°C)	20	26	17	24	30	15	18
Ice cream sales	35	39	27	36	45	25	32
	(20, 35)	(26, 39)	(17, 27)	(24, 36)	(30, 45)	(15, 25)	(18, 32)

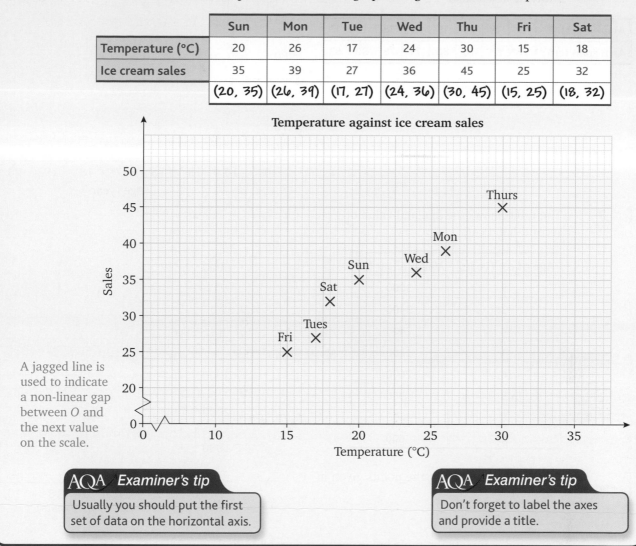

Temperature against ice cream sales

A jagged line is used to indicate a non-linear gap between O and the next value on the scale.

AQA *Examiner's tip*

Usually you should put the first set of data on the horizontal axis.

AQA *Examiner's tip*

Don't forget to label the axes and provide a title.

Practise... 8.1 Plotting points on a scatter graph   G F E D C

1   Write down the values of the following points.

a   A   B   C   D   E   F
    ×   ×   ×   ×   ×   ×
   0   10   20   30   40   50

b   A   B C   D   E   F   G   H
    ×   × ×   ×   ×   ×   ×   ×
   0   20   40   60   80   100

c   500 ×H   d 160 ×H   e 4 ┐   f   A   B   C D   E   F G   H
       ×G   140 ×G   │ ×H   ×   ×   × ×   ×   × ×   ×
       ×F   ×F   3 ×G   0   1   2   3   4   5   6   7   8   9   10
   400 ×E   120 ×G   │ ×G
       ×E   100 ×E   3 ×F
   300 ×D   80 ×D   │ ×E
       ×D   ×C   2 ×D
       ×C   60 ×C   │ ×C
   200 ×B   40 ×B   1 ×B
       ×B   20   │ ×A
   100 ×A   0 ×A   0 ×A

G

F

2 The table shows the age and arm span of students in a school.

Age (years)	15	19	16	18	17	18	16	17
Arm span (cm)	78	84	76	80	71	78	80	83

Copy the axes and plot the points on the graph.

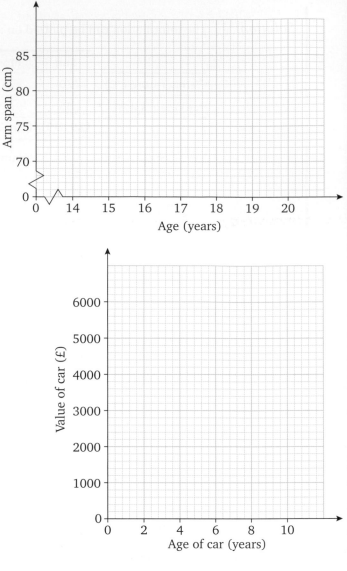

F
E

3 The table shows the age and value of second-hand cars.

Age of car (years)	Value of car (£)
5	3000
3	3400
4	2400
1	5200
6	2600
9	500
8	1600
10	600

Copy the axes and plot the points given in the table.

E

4 Copy and complete the table below, using the graph to find your values.

Point	A	B	C	D	E	F	G	H	I	J
Number of hours trained										
Fitness rating %										

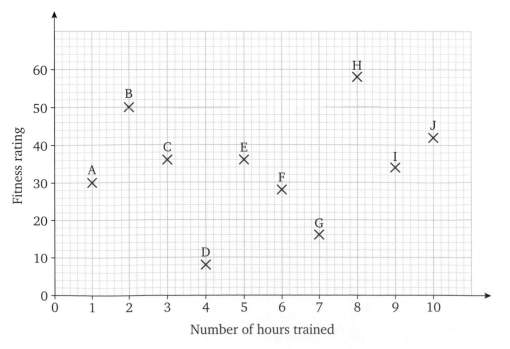

! 5 The following information shows the marks awarded to students on two exam papers.

French	31	14	65	28	55	59	44	77	40	49
Spanish	31	10	46	16	38	62	31	52	24	38

a Plot these points on a scatter graph.

b Tanya says that people who did well in Spanish also did well in French.
Is Tanya correct?
Give reasons for your answer.

6 The table shows the infant mortality rate and the life expectancy for 10 countries.

Country	Egypt	France	Germany	India	Japan	Kenya	Nigeria	Pakistan	UK	Zimbabwe
Infant mortality	28.4	3.4	4	32.3	2.8	56	95.7	66.9	4.9	33.9
Life expectancy	71.8	80.9	79.1	69.2	82.1	56.6	46.5	64.1	78.8	44.3

Infant mortality is the number of deaths per 1000 births.
Life expectancy is given in years.

a Draw a scatter graph to show this information.

b What do you notice?

Learn... 8.2 Interpreting scatter graphs

Correlation measures the relationship between two sets of data.

It is measured in terms of **type** and **strength** of correlation.

Type of correlation

Positive correlation	Negative correlation	Zero or no correlation
Positive correlation is where an increase in one set of data results in an increase in the other set of data.	**Negative correlation** is where an increase in one set of data results in a decrease in the other set of data.	**Zero or no correlation** is where there is no obvious relationship between the two sets of data.

Example:
Temperature against ice cream sales. As the temperature increases, the number of ice cream sales increases.

Example:
Temperature against sales of coats. As the temperature increases, the sales of coats decreases.

Example:
Temperature against toothpaste sales. There is no obvious relationship between temperature and toothpaste sales.

Strength of correlation

Strong correlation	Weak correlation	
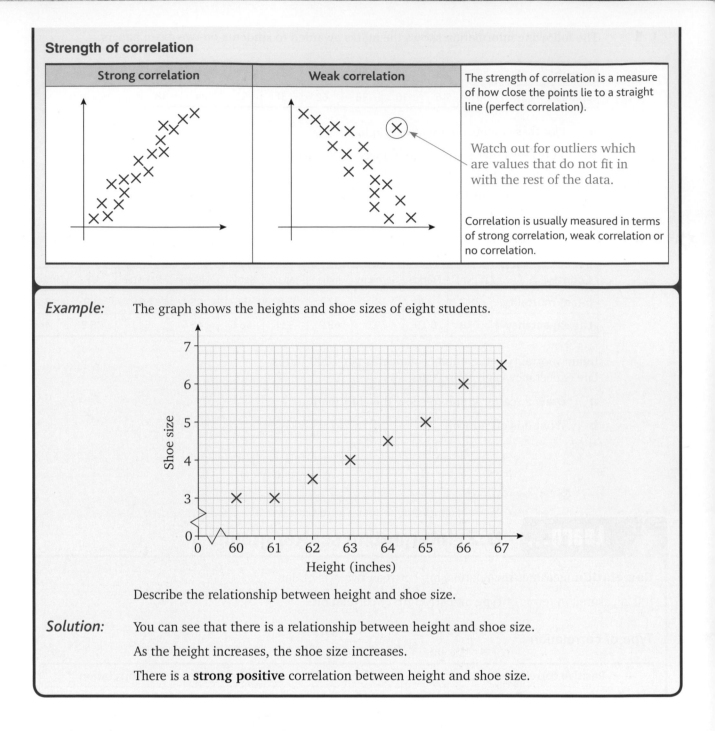		The strength of correlation is a measure of how close the points lie to a straight line (perfect correlation). Watch out for outliers which are values that do not fit in with the rest of the data. Correlation is usually measured in terms of strong correlation, weak correlation or no correlation.

Example: The graph shows the heights and shoe sizes of eight students.

Describe the relationship between height and shoe size.

Solution: You can see that there is a relationship between height and shoe size.

As the height increases, the shoe size increases.

There is a **strong positive** correlation between height and shoe size.

Practise... 8.2 Interpreting scatter graphs *k!*   G F E D C

E
D

1 For each of the following:

a describe the type and strength of correlation

b write a sentence explaining the relationship between the two sets of data (for example, as the hours of sunshine increase so do the sales of iced drinks).

i The hours of sunshine and the sales of iced drinks.

ii The number of cars on a road and the average speed.

iii The distance travelled and the amount of petrol used.

iv The cost of a house and the number of bedrooms.

v The amount of sunshine and the sale of umbrellas.

2 For each of these scatter graphs:

   a   describe the type and strength of correlation

   b   write a sentence explaining the relationship between the two sets of data.

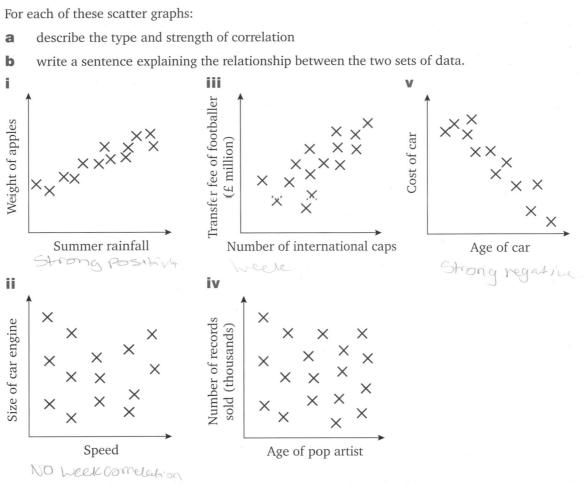

i

Weight of apples / Summer rainfall

Strong positive

iii

Transfer fee of footballer (£ million) / Number of international caps

weak

v

Cost of car / Age of car

Strong negative

ii

Size of car engine / Speed

No weak correlation

iv

Number of records sold (thousands) / Age of pop artist

3 The table shows the ages and arm spans of seven students in a school.

Age (years)	16	13	13	10	18	10	15
Arm span (inches)	62	57	59	57	64	55	61

   a   Represent the data on a scatter graph.

   b   Describe the type and strength of correlation.

   c   Write a sentence explaining the relationship between the two sets of data.

4 The table shows the hours of sunshine and rainfall in 10 seaside towns.

Sunshine (hours)	Rainfall (mm)
650	11
400	30
530	28
640	11
520	24
550	20
480	26
600	15
550	16
525	23

   a   Represent the data on a scatter graph.

   b   Describe the type and strength of correlation.

   c   Write a sentence explaining the relationship between the two sets of data.

D

5 For each graph, write down two variables that might fit the relationship.

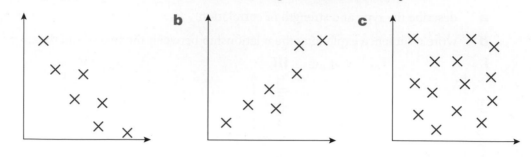

a   **b**   **c**

6 The scatter graph shows the ages and shoe sizes of a group of people.

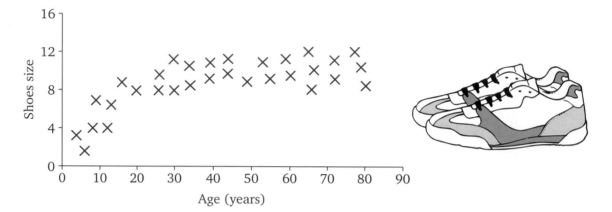

a Describe the type and strength of correlation.

b Give a reason for your answer.

7 Ron is investigating the fat content and the calorie values of food at his local fast-food restaurant.

He collects the following information.

	Fat (g)	Calories
Hamburger	9	260
Cheeseburger	12	310
Chicken nuggets	24	420
Fish sandwich	18	400
Medium fries	16	350
Medium cola	0	210
Milkshake	26	1100
Breakfast	46	730

a Describe the correlation between fat and calories.

b Does the relationship hold for all the different foods? Give a reason for your answer.

Hint

If you are asked to describe correlation you should draw a scatter graph first and then describe the type and strength of correlation.

Learn... 8.3 Lines of best fit

A **line of best fit** is drawn to represent the relationship between two sets of data on a scatter graph.

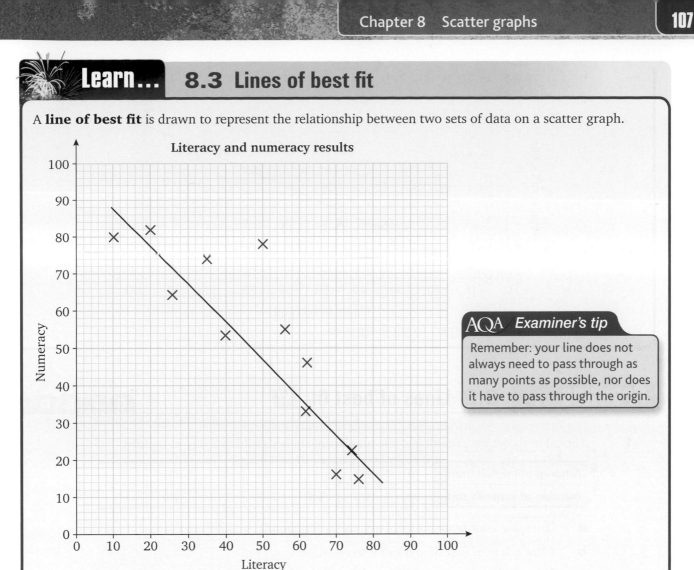

AQA Examiner's tip

Remember: your line does not always need to pass through as many points as possible, nor does it have to pass through the origin.

In this example, one of the values does not seem to fit the rest of the data.

This is called an **outlier** or rogue value.

Ignore these values when drawing a line of best fit.

You should draw the line of best fit so that:

- it gives a general trend for all of the data on the scatter graph
- it gives an idea of the strength and type of correlation
- there are roughly equal numbers of points above and below the line.

You can use the line of best fit to estimate missing data.

A line of best fit should only be drawn where the correlation is strong.

AQA Examiner's tip

When you are drawing your line of best fit, you will usually have a 'corridor of success'. This means that if your line of best fit falls within this 'corridor', you are correct.

Example:

The graph shows the number of hours' revision and the number of GCSE passes for 10 students.

Draw a line of best fit.

Dinah studies for 60 hours. How many GCSE passes is she likely to get?

Solution:

By drawing the line of best fit you can use the graph to estimate the number of GCSE passes.

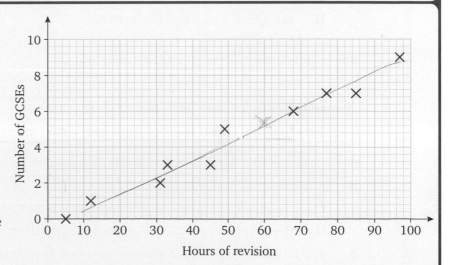

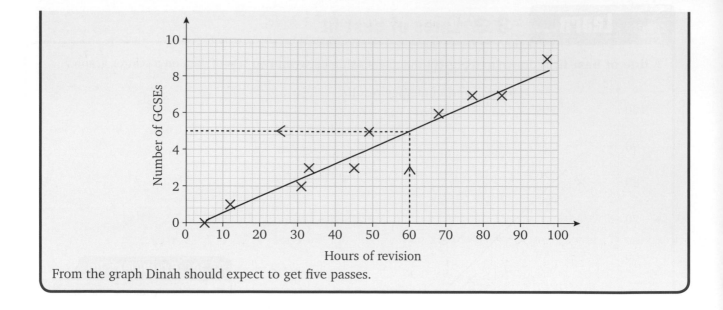

From the graph Dinah should expect to get five passes.

Practise... 8.3 Lines of best fit k!

D

1 The table shows the rainfall and the number of sunbeds sold in a day at a resort.

Amount of rainfall (mm)	0	1	2	5	6	9	11
Number of sunbeds sold	380	320	340	210	220	110	60

a Draw a scatter graph to represent this information.

b Draw a line of best fit and use it to estimate:

   i the number of sunbeds sold for 4 mm of rainfall

   ii the amount of rainfall if 100 sunbeds are sold.

2 The table shows the age and value of seven second-hand cars of the same model.

Age of car (years)	2	1	4	7	10	9	8
Value of car (£)	4200	4700	2800	1900	400	1100	2100

a Draw a scatter graph to represent this information.

b Draw a line of best fit and use it to estimate:

   i the value of a car if it is 7.5 years old

   ii the age of a car if its value is £3700.

3 Rob collects information on the temperature and the number of visitors to an art gallery.

Temperature (°C)	15	25	16	18	19	22	24	23	17	20	26	20
Number of visitors	720	180	160	620	510	400	310	670	720	530	180	420

a Draw a scatter graph to represent this information.

b Estimate:

   i the number of people if the temperature is 24°C

   ii the temperature if 350 people visit the art gallery.

c Rob is sure that two sets of data are incorrect. Identify these two sets of data on your graph.

⚠ **4**   Readings of two variables, *A* and *B*, are shown in the table.

A	1	2	3	4	5	6	7	0.8	2.1	3.2	3.9	5.1	6.2	7.1
B	1.8	8.8	20	33	48	73	95	2	9	18	31	49	72	98

a   Draw a scatter graph to represent the data.

b   Describe the correlation between the two sets of data.

c   Draw a curve of best fit and use this to estimate:

   i   the value of *B* if *A* = 2.5

   ii   the value of *A* if *B* = 64

⚙ **5**   The table shows the actual age and reading age of six girls and six boys in a class.

Girls	Ann	Bano	Carrie	Dianne	Elseph	Florence
Actual age (months)	60	65	71	61	68	66
Reading age (months)	59	63	68	61	64	64

Boys	Jack	Kevin	Leon	Manjeet	Nabeel	Oscar
Actual age (months)	63	66	70	64	67	69
Reading age (months)	58	60	64	59	63	65

a   What do you notice about the data?

b   If Paul is 68 months old, what is his likely reading age?

c   If Gail is 6 years old, what is her likely reading age?

d   Which student has a reading age which is the same as their actual age?

⚙ **6**   The table shows the distances from the equator and average temperatures for 12 cities.

The distance is measured in degrees from the equator.

The temperature is measured in degrees Celsius.

City	Distance from equator (°)	Average temp. (°C)
Bangkok	13	28
Beijing	39	12
Boston	42	9
Cairo	30	22
Cape Town	33	17
Copenhagen	55	8
Gibraltar	36	19
Istanbul	40	14
London	51	10
Moscow	55	4.2
Mumbai	18	27
Perth	32	18

a   What do you notice?

b   Dubai is 25° north of the equator.
Use these data to find the average temperature in Dubai.

c   What other factors might affect temperatures?

8 Assess

D

1 The information below shows the marks of eight students in history and geography.

Student	A	B	C	D	E	F	G	H
History	25	35	28	30	36	44	15	21
Geography	27	40	29	32	41	48	17	20

Draw a scatter graph to represent this information and comment on the relationship between the history and geography marks.

2 The following table shows the hours of TV watched and test marks for 10 students.

Student	1	2	3	4	5	6	7	8	9	10
TV hours	4	7	9	10	13	14	15	20	21	25
Test mark	9	90	74	30	74	66	95	38	35	30

a Draw a scatter graph to represent this information and comment on the relationship between the figures.

b Two students do not seem to 'fit the trend'.
Which ones are they? Explain why.

C

3 The tables show the relationship between the area (in thousands of km²) of some European countries and their populations (in millions) given to 2 s.f.

	Monaco	Malta	Jersey	Netherl.	UK	Germ.	Italy	Switz.	Andorra	Denm.
Area	0.0020	0.32	0.12	42	250	360	300	41	0.47	43
Population	0.030	0.40	0.090	16	60	83	58	7.3	0.068	5.4

	France	Austria	Turkey	Greece	Spain	Eire	Latvia	Sweden	Norway	Iceland
Area	550	84	780	130	500	70	65	450	320	100
Population	60	8.2	67	11	40	3.9	2.4	8.9	4.5	0.28

Draw a scatter graph of these data and comment on the graph.

4 The table shows the distance jumped in long jump trials and the leg length of the jumpers.

Leg length (cm)	71	73	74	75	76	79	82
Distance jumped (m)	3.2	3.1	3.3	4.1	3.9	4	4.8

a Draw a scatter graph to represent this information.

b Use a line of best fit to estimate:

i the leg length of an athlete who jumped a distance of 3.5 m

ii the distance jumped by an athlete with a leg length of 85 cm.

c Explain why one of those estimates is more reliable than the other.

Learn... 9.1 Describing probability

Probability words

Probability is all about how likely a particular **outcome** is.

Words can be used to describe probability.

The words you need to know are:

Impossible   an outcome that could not happen
              e.g. a cow passes GCSE English

Unlikely   an outcome that most of the time would not happen
              e.g. it snows in May in London

Evens   an outcome that has an equal chance of happening or not
              e.g. a **fair** coin lands showing heads

Likely   an outcome that most of the time would happen
              e.g. you have a hot meal during the day

Certain   an outcome that will always happen
              e.g. you will be older next year than you are now.

AQA *Examiner's tip*

If a question in the exam requires the use of words to describe probability, then you will be specifically asked to use words such as impossible and unlikely.

Other words can sometimes be added to these such as very unlikely and very likely.

A very unlikely outcome is one which is hardly ever going to happen but is not actually impossible, e.g. it will not rain in England for a whole month.

Probability scales

Numerical values for probability give more information than the probability words.

- An outcome that is impossible has a probability of 0.
- An outcome that is certain has a probability of 1.
- All other probability values lie between 0 and 1.

Fractions or decimals are the best way of showing probabilities.

Percentages are also sometimes used.

AQA *Examiner's tip*

Never use words such as 3 out of 10, or ratios such as 3 : 10, to describe probability. This always scores no marks. You must use fractions ($\frac{3}{10}$), decimals (0.3) or percentages (30%).

A **probability scale** can be used to show probability words and values.

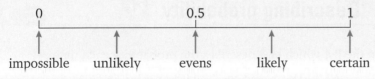

```
0                    0.5                    1
↑         ↑          ↑          ↑          ↑
impossible  unlikely   evens      likely    certain
```

Example: On a probability scale, place an arrow to indicate the probability of each **event**.

W   you get an even number when you roll an ordinary fair dice

X   you get wet the next time you have a shower

Y   you write a book when you are asleep

Z   your teacher's birthday is in a month beginning with J

AQA *Examiner's tip*

The words ordinary fair dice are used in exams to indicate it is a six-sided dice numbered 1, 2, 3, 4, 5, 6 with each score equally likely.

Solution:
```
0                    0.5                    1
↑         ↑          ↑                     ↑
Y         Z          W                     X
```

W   when you roll an ordinary fair dice there is an equal chance of getting an even number or not getting an even number so the probability is 0.5

X   you will always get wet when you have a shower so the probability is 1

Y   it is impossible to write a book when you are asleep so the probability is 0

Z   there are only three months in the year which begin with J so your teacher's birthday is unlikely to be in a month beginning with J

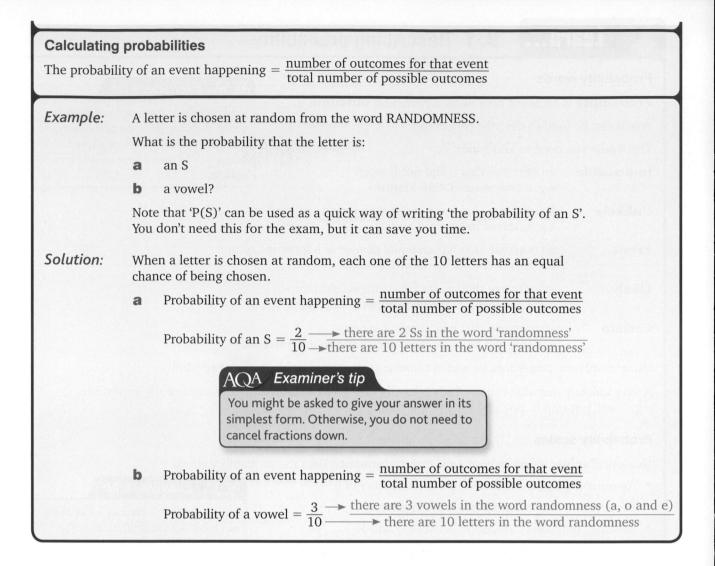

Calculating probabilities

The probability of an event happening = $\dfrac{\text{number of outcomes for that event}}{\text{total number of possible outcomes}}$

Example: A letter is chosen at random from the word RANDOMNESS.

What is the probability that the letter is:

a   an S

b   a vowel?

Note that 'P(S)' can be used as a quick way of writing 'the probability of an S'. You don't need this for the exam, but it can save you time.

Solution: When a letter is chosen at random, each one of the 10 letters has an equal chance of being chosen.

a   Probability of an event happening = $\dfrac{\text{number of outcomes for that event}}{\text{total number of possible outcomes}}$

Probability of an S = $\dfrac{2}{10}$ → there are 2 Ss in the word 'randomness'
→ there are 10 letters in the word 'randomness'

AQA *Examiner's tip*

You might be asked to give your answer in its simplest form. Otherwise, you do not need to cancel fractions down.

b   Probability of an event happening = $\dfrac{\text{number of outcomes for that event}}{\text{total number of possible outcomes}}$

Probability of a vowel = $\dfrac{3}{10}$ → there are 3 vowels in the word randomness (a, o and e)
→ there are 10 letters in the word randomness

Practise... 9.1 Describing probability 🄺   G F E D C

G

1   Choose the word from the list which best describes the probability each time.

   IMPOSSIBLE   UNLIKELY   EVENS   LIKELY   CERTAIN

a   You will be younger on your next birthday. *impossible*

b   It will be sunny on Christmas Day this year. *unlikely*

c   A black counter is taken out of a bag with 10 black and 10 white counters. *Evens*

d   You will marry an earwig when you are older.

2   Write down a statement to do with sport that is:

a   impossible (e.g. someone will run a mile in under a minute)

b   unlikely

c   likely

d   certain.

3 Make a copy of this probability scale.

```
0                    0.5                   1
└─────────────────────┴─────────────────────┘
```

Put arrows on the scale with letters a, b, c, and d for the events in Question 1.

4 An ordinary fair dice is rolled.

Find the probability of rolling each of the following.

a A five **c** A number less than 4

b A one **d** An odd number

AQA *Examiner's tip*

> Use fractions for answers on questions like these (Q4 and Q5). Decimals or percentages will make it far harder to score marks for accuracy.

5 A card is picked at random from a standard pack of 52 cards.

Find the probability of picking the following.

a A red card

b A black nine

c An ace

d The six of clubs

Hint

> A pack of cards has two red suits, hearts and diamonds, and two black suits, clubs and spades. Every suit has an ace, 2, 3, 4, 5, 6, 7, 8, 9, 10, jack, queen and king.

6 Quinlan has a set of cards numbered 1 to 100.

He picks one of these cards at random.

Find the probability of picking the following.

a A card with 34 on it **c** A card with a 9 on it

b A card with a number greater than 80 on it **d** A card without a 9 on it

7 Ross has 5 red marbles and 11 white marbles in a bag.

a If he picks a marble at random, what is the probability that it is red?

b What is the probability that it is not red?

c Jamie adds 4 black marbles to the bag and says 'The probability of getting a black marble is $\frac{4}{16}$'
Explain why he is wrong.

d What is the probability of picking a black marble from the bag?
Give your answer in its simplest form.

8 Jack has 30 marbles. Some are blue, some are yellow and some are grey.

He picks a marble at random.

The probability that he will pick a blue marble is 0.4
The probability that he will pick a yellow marble is 0.1

a How many blue marbles does he have?

b How many yellow marbles does he have?

c What is the probability that he will pick a grey marble?

9 There are some discs in a large bag.

There are three times as many black discs as blue.

There are twice as many blue discs as red.

A disc is taken from the bag at random.

What is the probability of picking a red disc at random?

Learn... 9.2 Combining events

Sometimes more than one event can happen at the same time.

You can use lists or **two-way tables** to help you work out these probabilities.

A table showing all possible outcomes is known as a **sample space diagram**. In the exam this sort of diagram will always be referred to as a two-way table.

AQA Examiner's tip

In the exam this sort of diagram will always be referred to as a two-way table.

Example: Tracey buys a drink and an ice cream from a shop.

The drinks available are Orange juice (O), Lemonade (L) and Water (W).

The ice creams available are Vanilla (V), Strawberry (S) and Chocolate (C).

a Make a list of the possible combinations of drink and ice cream.

b Show the same information in a table.

c Find the probability of Tracey buying:

   i lemonade and strawberry ice cream

   ii orange juice and an ice cream other than vanilla.

d What assumptions do you make for these probabilities?

Solution: **a** Be systematic (this means try to use an organised method) and list the options by letter.

     OV   OS   OC   LV   LS   LC   WV   WS   WC

b Using a two-way table reduces the chances of missing one out.

AQA Examiner's tip

Remember to be systematic when you complete a two-way table in an exam. This will help you to avoid making mistakes and to work out the correct probabilities.

	Vanilla	Strawberry	Chocolate
Orange juice	OV	OS	OC
Lemonade	LV	LS	LC
Water	WV	WS	WC

c **i** The table shows there are nine possible combinations of drink and ice cream.

Lemonade and strawberry ice cream is one of these nine.

Probability $= \dfrac{1}{9}$

ii The options are OS or OC.

This is two out of the nine options.

Probability $= \dfrac{2}{9}$

d You have to assume that all the options are equally likely to be chosen.

This means that Tracey must like all the options and not have a favourite.

In real life this is unlikely.

Tracey does not like vanilla ice cream.

Vanilla ice cream now has no chance of being picked and is not an equally likely choice.

Practise...   9.2 Combining events    G F E D C

1 Trevor is having lunch at his office restaurant. He chooses a sandwich and a piece of fruit.

The sandwich choice is ham (H), beef (B), cheese (C) or egg (E).

The fruit choice is apple (A), orange (O) or pear (P).

a Make a list of the combinations of sandwich and fruit Trevor could choose.

b Show this information in a table.

c What is the probability that Trevor chooses the following?

    i a ham sandwich and an apple

    ii an egg sandwich

d What assumption did you make in answering part **c**?

e Do you think this assumption is valid? Explain your answer.

> **Hint**
>
> Remember to be systematic. First list all combinations where ham is the sandwich choice, then all when beef is the sandwich choice, and so on.

2 Two ordinary fair dice are rolled.

The scores on each dice are added together.

a Copy and complete the two-way table.

b Use the table to find the probability that the total is:

    i 2   **iii** more than 9

    ii 4   **iv** even.

	1	2	3	4	5	6
1	2	3	4	5		
2	3	4	5			
3	4	5				
4	5					
5						
6						

3 Two ordinary fair dice are rolled.

The scores on each dice are multiplied together.

a Construct a two-way table to show all the possible totals.

b Use the table to find the probability that the total is:

    i 1   **iii** less than 10

    ii 12   **iv** odd.

4 Lucy says that if you flip two coins, the possible outcomes are two heads, two tails or one of each. She therefore decides that the probability of getting two heads is $\frac{1}{3}$

Explain why Lucy is wrong.

5 Use your answer to Question 4 to help in this question.

Three coins are flipped.

What is the probability of getting two heads and a tail in any order?

6 Amy is trying to persuade her parents to double her pocket money if, when she rolls two dice, the total is a prime number.

Her parents suggest the money is doubled when the total is a square number.

Should Amy accept her parents' suggestion?

7 Two dice are rolled and their scores added to give a total.

The probability of a total of X is $\frac{1}{9}$

What are the two possible values for X?

> **Hint**
>
> You may find your answer to Q2 helpful in answering this.

Learn... 9.3 Mutually exclusive events k!

Mutually exclusive events are events that cannot happen at the same time.

For example, the following events are mutually exclusive.

* Getting a head and getting a tail when a coin is flipped once.
* Getting a three and getting an even number when a dice is rolled once.
* Sleeping and running the marathon at the same time.
* Flying a plane and swimming the English Channel at the same time.

Other events are not mutually exclusive and can happen at the same time.

For example, the following events are not mutually exclusive.

* Getting a four and getting an even number when a dice is rolled.
* Getting a red card and getting an Ace when a card is taken from a pack.
* Driving a car and listening to the radio.
* Eating a meal and watching TV.

AQA **Examiner's tip**

In the examination the words 'mutually exclusive' will not be used.

However, you need to understand how events happening at the same time affect probabilities.

In any given probability situation, the total probability is always 1.

More accurately, you can say that if mutually exclusive events cover all the possibilities the sum of their probabilities total 1.

Example: 10 discs are placed in a bag.

They are labelled X1, X2, X3, X4, Y1, Y2, Y3, Y4, Z1 and Z2.

One disc is picked at random.

Work out the probability of picking the following.

a   A disc with an X on it

b   A disc without an X on it

c   A disc with a 3 on it

d   A disc without a 3 on it

e   A disc with an X or a 3 on it

Solution: **a**   Probability of an event happening $= \dfrac{\text{number of outcomes for that event}}{\text{total number of possible outcomes}}$

Probability of picking an X $= \dfrac{4}{10}$ → there are 4 discs with an X on
→ there are 10 discs altogether

b   Probability of an event happening $= \dfrac{\text{number of outcomes for that event}}{\text{total number of possible outcomes}}$

Probability of not picking an X $= \dfrac{6}{10}$ → there are 6 discs without an X on
→ there are 10 discs altogether

Alternatively, if mutually exclusive events cover all the possibilities, their probabilities total 1.

Here every disc has to be either an X or not an X.

The probability of picking an X + the probability of not picking an X = 1.

So, the probability of not picking an X = 1 − the probability of picking an X.

Probability of not picking an X $= 1 - \dfrac{4}{10} = \dfrac{6}{10}$

c Probability of an event happening $= \dfrac{\text{number of outcomes for that event}}{\text{total number of possible outcomes}}$

Probability of a 3 $= \dfrac{2}{10}$ → there are 2 discs with a 3 on
→ there are 10 discs altogether

d $1 - \dfrac{2}{10} = \dfrac{8}{10}$ (probability of not picking a 3 is $1 -$ probability of picking a 3)

e The probability of picking a disc with an X or a 3 on is not $\dfrac{4}{10} + \dfrac{2}{10}$

This would count the X3 disc twice!

This confirms that only mutually exclusive probabilities can be added.

Here you must use the list. Out of the ten possible outcomes, there are five discs with either an X or a 3 on them.

X1, X2, X3, X4, Y3

So the probability is $\dfrac{5}{10}$

> **AQA Examiner's tip**
>
> None of the answers in the example are simplified, as simplest form was not asked for.
>
> If the question in the exam does not ask you to provide an answer in its simplest form, then there is no need to cancel.

Practise... 9.3 Mutually exclusive events k!

1 Which of these pairs of dice events could not happen at the same time?

a Roll a 1 and roll a number less than 5

b Roll a 2 and roll an odd number

c Roll an even number and roll an odd number

d Roll a number more than 3 and a number less than 4

2 The probability that Georgina will wear black on a Saturday is 0.95

What is the probability that Georgina will not wear black on a Saturday?

3 The probability that Mike will have fish and chips for dinner is 0.07

What is the probability that Mike will not have fish and chips for dinner?

4 The probability that Toni will not drink tea at work is 0.001

What is the probability that Toni will drink tea at work?

5 Losalot Town are playing in a football tournament.

Here are some probabilities for the outcome of their opening match.

Complete the table.

Probability of winning	Probability of drawing	Probability of losing
$\dfrac{1}{10}$	$\dfrac{1}{5}$	

> **AQA Examiner's tip**
>
> Remember that you can use a calculator in this unit.
> There is no point trying to answer these questions without one!

6 A bag contains coloured discs.

Each disc also has a letter on it.

There are 5 red discs D, E, F, G and H.

There are 8 blue discs D, E, F, G, H, I, J and K.

There are 2 yellow discs D and E.

Work out the probability of picking a disc that:

a is red

b has an E on it

c does not have an E on it

d is red or has an E on it

e is yellow or has an F on it

f is blue or has an H on it.

7 Errol goes out to buy a new sweatshirt.

The probability that he buys it from Supershirts is $\frac{9}{20}$

The probability that he buys it from BestSweats is $\frac{2}{5}$

What is the probability that he buys it from either one of these stores?

8 A local council is looking at traffic flow at a busy junction.

The approach to the junction has three lanes.

The table shows the probability of a car being in a given lane.

Lane	Probability
Left	0.39
Centre	0.06
Right	

a Work out the probability of a car being in the right hand lane.

The probability of a car containing a single person is 0.77

b Explain why the probability of a car with a single person being in the centre is **not** 0.83

c Complete this table.

Lane	Single person	More than one person
Left	0.33	
Centre	0.05	
Right		

> **Hint**
>
> The events 'a car with a single person in' and 'a car with more than one person in' are mutually exclusive.

9 Of the people attending a festival, one is chosen at random to win a prize.

The probability the chosen person is male is 0.515

The probability the chosen person is married is 0.048

The probability the chosen person is a married male is 0.029

What is the probability the chosen person is an unmarried female?

10 A bag contains shapes which are coloured.

The probability of a red square is 0.2

The probability of a red shape is 0.2

Write down one fact about the shapes in the bag.

Learn... 9.4 Relative frequency

The probabilities so far have all been theoretical probabilities.

Theoretical probability is the probability of an event based on expectation (or theory).

A probability experiment is a test in which a number of **trials** are performed.

Experimental probability is the probability of an event based on testing (or experiment).
The experimental probability is also called the **relative frequency**.

Example: Niles rolls an ordinary dice 120 times.

His results are shown in the table.

Score	1	2	3	4	5	6
Frequency	17	18	24	22	25	14

a   Work out the relative frequency for each score.

b   How many of each score would you expect if the dice was fair?

c   Do you think the dice is fair? Explain your answer.

d   Estimate the probability of scoring a two on this dice.

Solution: a   Relative frequency of an event $= \dfrac{\text{number of times an event has happened}}{\text{total number of trials}}$

The score of 1 happened 17 times out of 120.

This means the relative frequency of a 1 is $\dfrac{17}{120}$

The remaining relative frequencies are shown in the extended table.

Score	1	2	3	4	5	6
Frequency	17	18	24	22	25	14
Relative Frequency	$\frac{17}{120}$	$\frac{18}{120}$	$\frac{24}{120}$	$\frac{22}{120}$	$\frac{25}{120}$	$\frac{14}{120}$

b   You would expect **about** 20 of each number if the dice is fair $\left(120 \times \dfrac{1}{6}\right)$.

(You can rarely get exactly what you expect in an actual experiment.)

c   The dice looks like it is **not** fair.

The values are reasonably close to the expected value of 20.

It is highly unlikely it would be exactly 20.

Indeed if the same experiment is repeated it would probably give different results even if the dice was fair.

d   The experimental results give an estimate of the probability of rolling a 2 as $\dfrac{18}{120}$

Since these results are close to the expected outcome, the dice appears to be fair.

On a fair dice the theoretical probability of rolling a 2 is actually $\dfrac{1}{6}$

AQA *Examiner's tip*

Relative frequencies should always be given as fractions or decimals. Giving the frequencies will often score zero.

The more times you carry out an experiment, the more reliable the results will be.

What if Niles had only rolled the dice 20 times?

It would be impossible to tell if the dice was **biased** or to use the results for estimating.

This idea can be shown on a relative frequency graph.

Example: When Niles rolled the dice, he kept a record of the number of 2s every 10 throws.

Here are his results.

Number of throws	10	20	30	40	50	60	70	80	90	100	110	120
Number of 2s	1	5	8	10	10	12	13	13	15	15	16	18

a   Find the relative frequency after every 10 throws.

b   Draw a line graph to show these results.

c   What can you see from the graph?

Solution: **a**   After 10 throws there had been one 2 giving a relative frequency of $\frac{1}{10} = 0.1$

After 20 throws there had been five 2s giving a relative frequency of $\frac{5}{20} = 0.25 \dots$

Number of throws	10	20	30	40	50	60	70	80	90	100	110	120
Number of 2s	1	5	8	10	10	12	13	13	15	15	16	18
Relative frequency	0.1	0.25	0.27	0.25	0.2	0.2	0.19	0.16	0.17	0.15	0.15	0.15

b

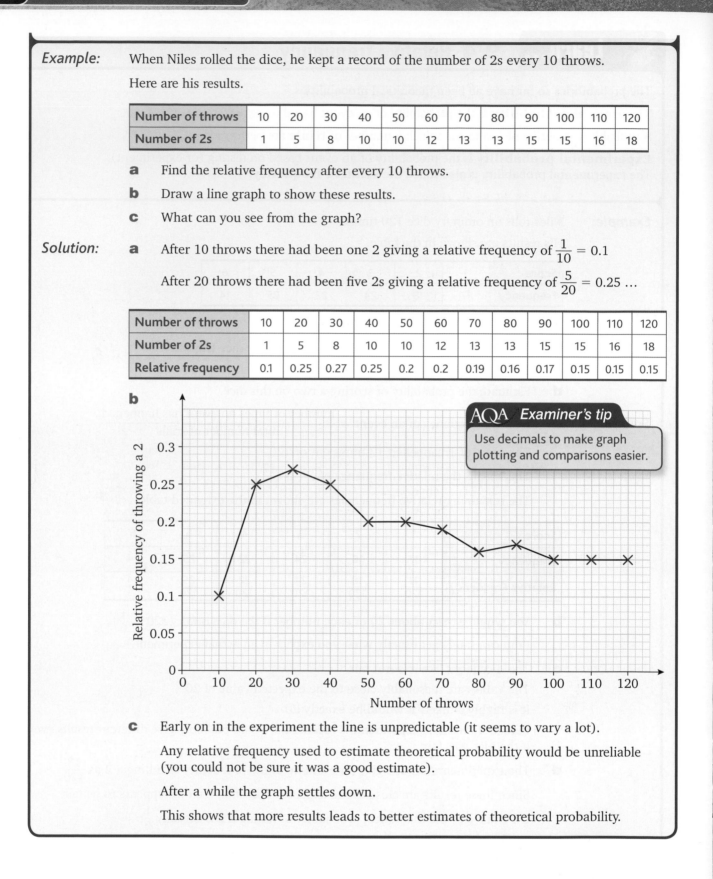

AQA *Examiner's tip*

Use decimals to make graph plotting and comparisons easier.

c   Early on in the experiment the line is unpredictable (it seems to vary a lot).

Any relative frequency used to estimate theoretical probability would be unreliable (you could not be sure it was a good estimate).

After a while the graph settles down.

This shows that more results leads to better estimates of theoretical probability.

Practise... 9.4 Relative frequency   🅚   G F E D C

E

1   A dice is rolled 100 times. A six appears on one quarter of these rolls.

What is the relative frequency of a six?

2   A spinner is spun 200 times. 'Red' appears 25 times.

What is the relative frequency of 'red'?

3   Alan rolls an ordinary fair dice 600 times.

  a   How many times would he expect to get a five?

  b   Would you expect to see exactly this number occurring?
         Give a reason for your answer.

4   Ruth flips a coin 240 times.

  a   How many times would she expect to get a tail?

  b   She actually gets 109 tails.
         Do you think the coin is biased?
         Give a reason for your answer.

5   A fair spinner with five equal divisions labelled A, B, C, D, E is spun 100 times.

  a   How many times would you expect it to land on A?

  b   How many times would you expect it to land on D?

  c   Julie spins the spinner 10 times and gets 2 As, 3 Bs, no Cs and 5 Ds.
         She says this shows the spinner is biased. Is she correct?
         Explain your answer.

6   Over a long period of time it is found that the probability of a faulty light bulb
       is 0.01

  a   How many light bulbs would you expect to be faulty in a batch of 500?

  b   One day, a light bulb checker finds 17 faulty bulbs.
         Estimate how many bulbs she has checked that day.

7   The table shows the frequency distribution after drawing a card from a pack
       40 times. The card is put back after each draw.

Results from 40 draws			
	Club	Heart	Diamond	Spade
Frequency	9	9	12	10

  a   What is the relative frequency of getting a heart?

  b   What is the relative frequency of getting a red card?

  c   What is the theoretical probability of getting a club?

  d   Ciaron says 'If you drew a card out 80 times you would probably get twice
         as many of each suit.' Explain why Ciaron is wrong.

8   Kali has a spinner with coloured sections of equal size.

  She wants to know the probability that her spinner
  lands on pink.

  She spins it 100 times and calculates the relative
  frequency of pink after every 10 spins.

  Her results are shown on the graph.

  a   Use the graph to calculate the number of times
         the spinner landed on pink:

    i   after the first 10 spins

    ii   after the first 50 spins.

  b   From the graph, estimate the probability of the
         spinner landing on pink.

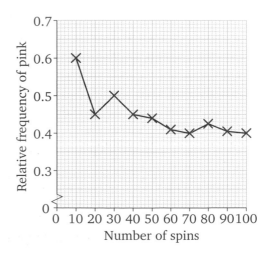

! **9**   Izzy is rolling a dice.

After every 10 throws she works out the relative frequency of a score of 1.

The diagram shows the relative frequency throughout the experiment.

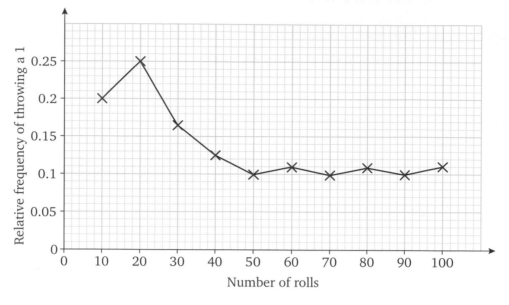

a   After 20 throws, how many 1s had there been?

b   How many 1s were there between the 21st and 50th throws?

c   Do you think this dice is biased? Explain your answer.

! **10**   The table shows the frequency distribution after throwing a dice 270 times.

Results from 270 throws of dice					
	1	**2**	**3**	**4**	**5**	**6**
Frequency	52	56	41	37	45	39

a   What is the relative frequency of getting a 2?

b   What is the relative frequency of getting a score greater than 4?

c   What is the relative frequency of getting an even number?

d   Ellie says the relative frequency of getting a score less than 3 is $\frac{149}{270}$
Is this correct? Explain your answer.

e   Which one of the frequencies is the same as the result you would expect
from theoretical probability?

? **11**   A fair spinner is made from a regular octagon.

Each of the eight sections of the spinner has one of the letters P, Q, R, S.

It is spun 240 times and the results are shown in the table.

Results from 240 spins			
P	**Q**	**R**	**S**
Frequency	34	62	88	56

How many times does each letter appear on the spinner?

9 Assess

1 Mark the probabilities of the events shown below on a probability scale like this one.

```
|_____|_____|
0                1/2               1
```

a The probability of obtaining a tail when a fair coin is flipped.

b The probability of scoring more than four when a fair six-sided dice is rolled.

c The probability of taking a green ball out of a bag containing 9 green and 3 red balls.

d The probability that you will need to breathe tomorrow.

e The probability that a card picked from a standard pack will be a heart.

f The probability that a number picked at random from the list: 1, 3, 5, 7, 9 will be even.

2 Work out the probability of:

a obtaining a 5 when an ordinary fair dice is rolled

b selecting an 8 from a standard pack of cards

c picking an even number from a bag containing the first 21 whole numbers

d picking an M from a bag containing the letters of the word ALUMINIUM.

3 Here are three of the longest words in the English language.

ANTIDISESTABLISHMENTARIANISM

FLOCCINUACINIHILIPILIFICATION

PNEUMONOULTRAMICROSCOPICSILICOVOLCANOCONIOSIS

A letter is picked at random from each of these words.
Which word has the greatest probabilty of having a letter I picked at random?

> **Hint**
> Use your calculator to convert to decimals.

4 In the UK the probability of being left handed is about 0.11

How many left-handed people would you expect to find in the following?

a A class of 33 children.

b A street of 132 people.

c A town of 55 000 people.

5 Two pentagonal spinners, each with the numbers 1 to 5, are spun and their outcomes added together to give a score.

a Draw a two-way table for the two spinners.

b Use your diagram to find:

   i the probability of a score of 4

   ii the probability of a score of 5

   iii the probability of a score of 9

   iv the most likely score.

c Repeat parts **a** and **b** for a score that is the outcomes **multiplied** together.

G
F

F

E

D

C

6 A fair six-sided dice is thrown 250 times and the following results obtained.

Score	1	2	3	4	5	6
Frequency	45	48	43	40	38	36

a What is the relative frequency of a score of 1?

b What is the relative frequency of a score of 6?

c What is the relative frequency of scoring more than 3?

d How do these data confirm that the dice is fair?

e Draw a new table with possible frequencies if this dice was thrown 6000 times.

7 The table below shows the probabilities of selecting tickets from a bag.

The tickets are coloured yellow, black or green and numbered 1, 2, 3 or 4.

	1	2	3	4
Yellow	$\frac{1}{20}$	$\frac{1}{16}$	$\frac{3}{40}$	$\frac{1}{8}$
Black	$\frac{1}{10}$	$\frac{3}{40}$	0	$\frac{3}{40}$
Green	0	$\frac{1}{8}$	$\frac{3}{16}$	$\frac{1}{8}$

A ticket is taken at random from the bag.

Calculate the probability that:

a it is green and numbered 2

b it is black

c it is not green

d it is yellow or numbered 4.

8 A bag contains red, white, blue and green counters.
A counter is picked at random from the bag.
The probability of picking a red counter is 0.5
The probability of picking a white counter is 0.1
The probability of picking a red or blue counter is 0.7

What is the probability of picking a green counter?

9 In a game a play can choose to roll one dice or two dice.
The player needs to score 5 to win.

Should the player choose to throw one dice or two?

AQA Examination-style questions

1 The spinner has eight equal sections.

Each section of this spinner has the number 1, 2, 3 or 4 in it.

All the numbers appear on the spinner.

Copy the diagram and write the numbers in the sections so that:
1 is the most likely score
4 is the least likely score
2 and 3 are equally likely scores.

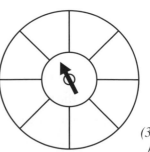

(3 marks)
AQA 2008

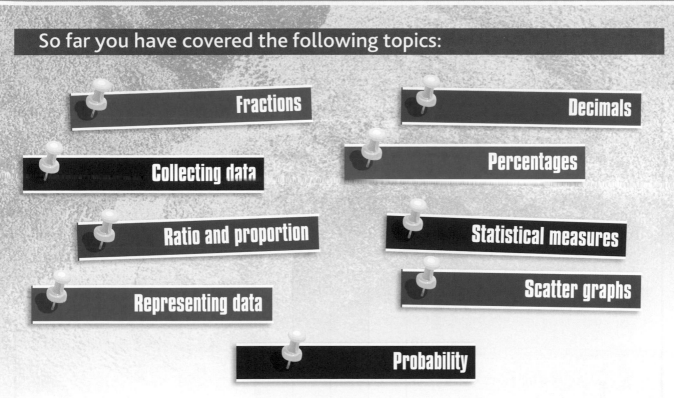

So far you have covered the following topics:

Fractions

Decimals

Collecting data

Percentages

Ratio and proportion

Statistical measures

Representing data

Scatter graphs

Probability

All these topics will be tested in this chapter and you will find a mixture of problem solving and functional questions. You won't always be told which bit of maths to use or what type a question is, so you will have to decide on the best method, just like in your exam.

Example: The length of 50 films is given in the table.

Length of film (min)	Frequency
$70 \leq l < 80$	19
$80 \leq l < 90$	22
$90 \leq l < 100$	7
$100 \leq l < 110$	2

Copy the graph below and draw a suitable diagram to show the data.

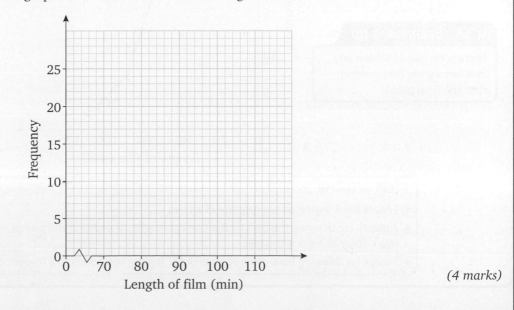

(4 marks)

Solution:

For this continuous data, the choices are to draw a frequency diagram or a frequency polygon.

Frequency diagram

For a frequency diagram, the height of each bar represents the frequency for each class interval. For continuous data, the bars are joined together.

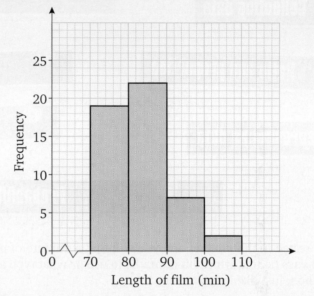

Frequency polygon

For a frequency polygon, plot the frequency values at the midpoint of each class interval. The points should be joined to create the frequency polygon.

For example, the midpoint of the first class is $\dfrac{70 + 80}{2} = 75$

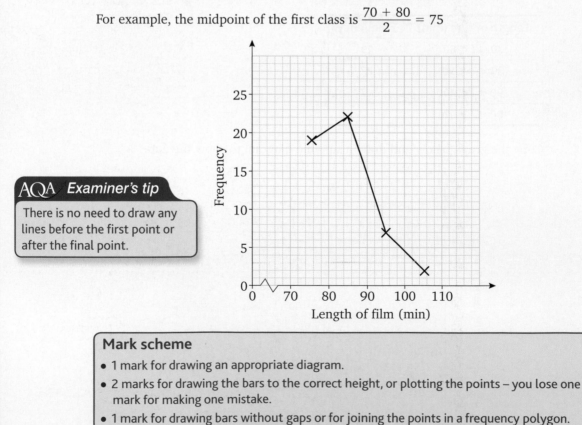

Mark scheme

- 1 mark for drawing an appropriate diagram.
- 2 marks for drawing the bars to the correct height, or plotting the points – you lose one mark for making one mistake.
- 1 mark for drawing bars without gaps or for joining the points in a frequency polygon.

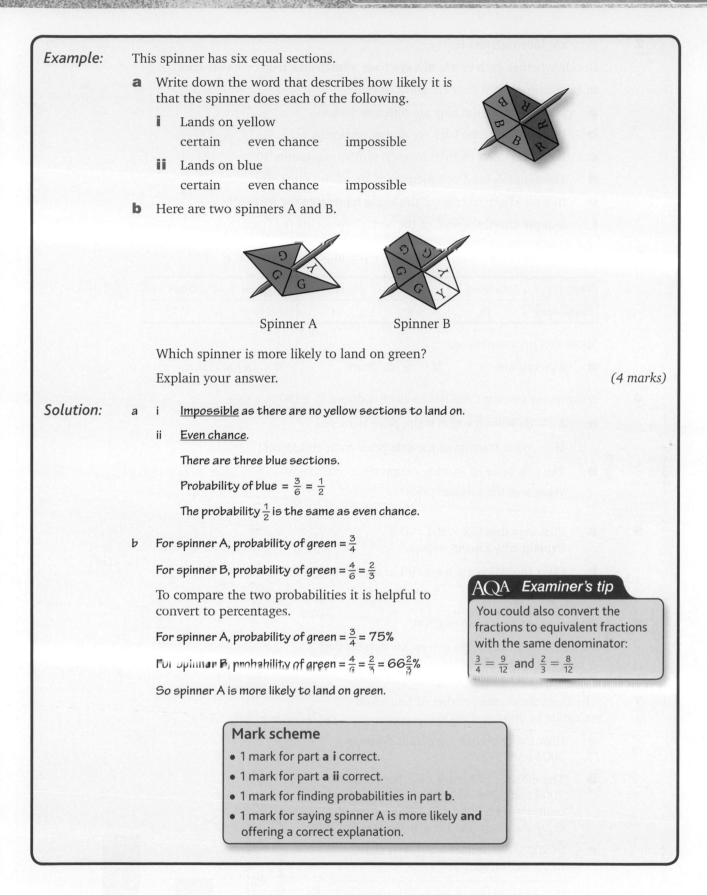

Example: This spinner has six equal sections.

a Write down the word that describes how likely it is that the spinner does each of the following.

i Lands on yellow

certain   even chance   impossible

ii Lands on blue

certain   even chance   impossible

b Here are two spinners A and B.

Spinner A   Spinner B

Which spinner is more likely to land on green?

Explain your answer.

(4 marks)

Solution: **a** **i** <u>Impossible</u> as there are no yellow sections to land on.

ii <u>Even chance</u>.

There are three blue sections.

Probability of blue $= \frac{3}{6} = \frac{1}{2}$

The probability $\frac{1}{2}$ is the same as even chance.

b For spinner A, probability of green $= \frac{3}{4}$

For spinner B, probability of green $= \frac{4}{6} = \frac{2}{3}$

To compare the two probabilities it is helpful to convert to percentages.

For spinner A, probability of green $= \frac{3}{4} = 75\%$

For spinner B, probability of green $= \frac{4}{6} = \frac{2}{3} = 66\frac{2}{3}\%$

So spinner A is more likely to land on green.

> **AQA** *Examiner's tip*
>
> You could also convert the fractions to equivalent fractions with the same denominator:
>
> $\frac{3}{4} = \frac{9}{12}$ and $\frac{2}{3} = \frac{8}{12}$

> **Mark scheme**
>
> • 1 mark for part **a i** correct.
> • 1 mark for part **a ii** correct.
> • 1 mark for finding probabilities in part **b**.
> • 1 mark for saying spinner A is more likely **and** offering a correct explanation.

Consolidation Kj

1 **a** Write 0.75 as a fraction.

b Write $\frac{9}{100}$ as a percentage.

c Write two fifths as a decimal.

d Write $\frac{11}{100}$ as a decimal.

e Write down a fraction between $\frac{1}{5}$ and $\frac{2}{5}$

G
F
E

2 Here are four statements.

Decide whether each one is **always true**, **sometimes true** or **never true**.

In each case explain your choice of answer.

a In a bar chart, the bars are different widths.

b In a bar chart, the bars are drawn vertically.

c In the key for a pictogram, each symbol represents 10.

d The symbols used in a pictogram are all the same size.

e In a pie chart, the size of the angle represents the frequency.

f In a pie chart, the area of the sector represents the frequency.

3 The table shows the sales of different types of tea.

Tea	Ordinary	Apple	Blackcurrant	Lemon	Other
Frequency	18	8	4	5	1

Show this information as:

a a pictogram   **b** a bar chart   **c** a pie chart.

4 A computer costing £900 has its price reduced by £150 in a sale.

a i By what fraction is the price reduced?

ii What fraction of the sale price is the reduction?

b The sale price of another computer in the sale was £600 after a reduction of $\frac{1}{4}$
What was the original price?

5 **a** Ellie says that $0.2 \times 0.4 = 0.8$
Explain why Ellie is wrong.

b Copy this calculation and fill in the missing number.
$0.3 \times \square = 6$

6 Amir is given a pay rise of £500.

He says this is only a 2% rise on his current pay.

How much will Amir earn after the pay rise?

7 The chart shows the number of houses on an estate in 2004 and 2006.

a How many houses were built between 2004 and 2006?

b The number of houses built between 2006 and 2008 was only $\frac{2}{3}$ of the number built between 2004 and 2006.
Copy the chart and draw in the bar for 2008.

c In 2003, the builder was given the following target:

> ratio of the number of houses in 2004 : number of houses in 2010 must not be less than 1 : 2.1

Between 2008 and 2009 he built 7 houses.

Do you think the builder is likely to meet his target?

You **must** show working to justify your answer.

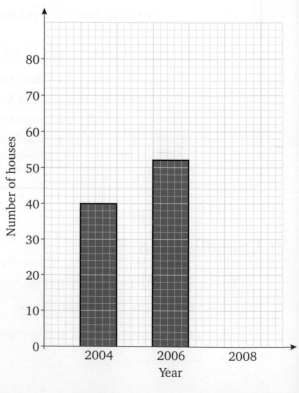

8 A gym club has 18 male and 12 female members.

   a   Julie says that the fraction of female members is $\frac{12}{18}$
       Is Julie correct? Give a reason for your answer.

   b   20 new members join the club.
       The ratio of male to female members is now 2 : 3
       How many of the new members were male?

9 Zafeer runs 400 m races.

He has taken part in 9 races so far and his mean time is 50.08 seconds.

His aim is to achieve a mean time under 50 seconds.

He has one race left to run.

What time must he run if he is to achieve his aim?

10 Prita starts with a number between 4 and 6.

She adds 0.2 to her number and then doubles the answer.

She repeats these two steps a number of times until she gets to 50.

What number does Prita start with?

11 Copy the diagram. Then connect each of the following to its proper description.
The first one has been done for you.

The age of lions at London Zoo
People's favourite cake at a show
Points scored in 10 darts matches
The weight of 12 newborn puppies
The favourite building of people in Britain
The average speed of train journeys into London
The number of hours spent driving per day
A person's shirt collar size
The cost of bread
Rainfall at a seaside resort

Quantitative and discrete
Qualitative
Quantitative and continuous

12 A hockey team have won $\frac{1}{2}$ of their matches and drawn $\frac{1}{4}$ of them.

They have lost six matches.

They are awarded two points for a win,
one point for a draw
and no points for a loss.

How many points have the team been awarded?

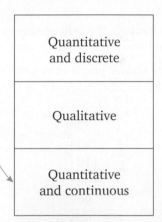

13 A recipe lists the following quantities of ingredients to make six scones.

   a   List the ingredients needed to make 12 scones.

   b   How much flour is needed for 15 scones?

   c   Write the ratio of flour : sultanas : butter : sugar
       in its simplest form.

Six scones ...

Self-raising flour	240 g
Salt	0.5 teaspoon
Sultanas	75 g
Butter	40 g
Caster sugar	25 g
Egg	1 large
Milk	20 ml

E
C

D

E
D
C

D

14 Andy and Roger have played each other at tennis 40 times.

Roger has won 60% of the games.

Andy has won three times more games on a hard court than on a grass court. 35% of the games have been played on a grass court.

All other games have been played on a hard court.

a Copy and complete the table.

	Number of wins for Andy	Number of wins for Roger
Played on grass court		
Played on hard court		

b Andy and Roger play their next match tomorrow.

If it is raining it will be played on a hard court.

If it is fine it will be played on a grass court.

What would Andy prefer?

Give a reason for your answer.

15 In football, the referee shows a player a yellow card for a bad foul and a red card when the player is sent off.

The scatter graph shows the number of red and yellow cards awarded by 12 referees labelled A to L in the Premier League for the 2008–2009 season.

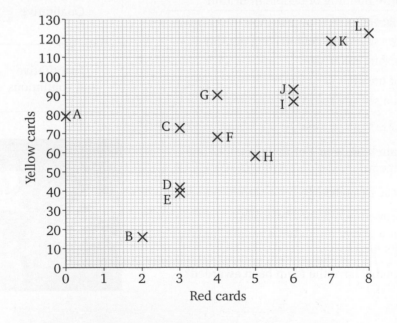

a One referee showed 8 times more yellow cards than red cards.
Which referee was this?

b The mean number of cards per match shown by G was 4.087 to 3 decimal places.
How many matches did G referee?

c Angie says, 'The more yellow cards a referee shows, the more red cards the referee shows.'
Comment on this statement.

16 A spinner has 10 equal sections.

Each section is red, blue or green.

All three colours are used at least once.

The probability of the spinner landing on green is the same as the probability of the spinner landing on blue.

The colour that the spinner is most likely to land on is red.

Show **two** ways that the spinner could be labelled.

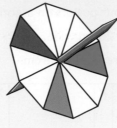 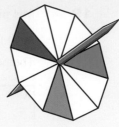

D

17 The table shows the engine sizes and maximum speeds of eight cars.

Engine size (cc)	Maximum speed (mph)
1100	80
1800	125
2900	142
1400	107
1300	96
1000	85
2500	135
2000	131

a Draw a scatter graph to show these results.

b Describe the relationship between a car's engine size and its maximum speed.

c Use a line of best fit to estimate:

i the maximum speed of a car with an engine size of 1500 cc

ii the engine size of a car whose maximum speed is 150 mph.

d Explain why your last answer might not be accurate.

18 Students at a college are asked to choose their favourite colour.

Their choices are shown in the pie chart.

D
G

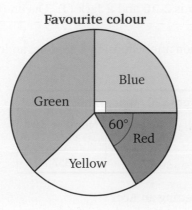

Favourite colour

A total of 45 students choose the colour blue.

Twice as many students choose green as yellow.
How many students choose green?

D
C

19 Mel pins up four posters on a noticeboard.

Each poster is 20 cm wide.

The posters overlap by 0.8 cm.

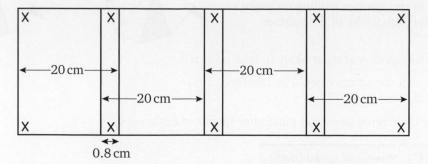

Work out the total width of the four posters on the noticeboard.

20 In a bingo club, 87% of the members are female.

a What percentage of members are male?

b The manager sends a voucher to every fourth name on the membership list.

He sends out 155 vouchers altogether.

What is the least number of members that the club has?

c The manager is thinking about closing the club on Mondays.

He gives a questionnaire about this to the first 10 males and the first 10 females to enter the club one Friday.

Is this a good sample to choose?

Give **two** reasons for your decision.

C

21 The mean of five numbers is 27.6

When the numbers are arranged in order the first two numbers are the same. The difference between each of the other numbers is always 2.

Work out the median.

22 An ordinary pack of cards has four suits called clubs, diamonds, spades and hearts. Each suit has an Ace, number cards 2–10 and a Jack (J), Queen (Q) and King (K). There are 52 cards in total.

The table shows the frequency distribution after choosing a card at random 520 times from a complete pack.

	Results from 520 random choices		
	Picture card (J, Q, K)	Ace	Number card
Frequency distribution	119	44	357

a What is the relative frequency of getting an Ace?

b Which of the results in the table is the closest to the result predicted by theoretical probability?

23 The table shows the time spent waiting at a clinic.

Time, t (minutes)	Frequency
$0 \leqslant t < 10$	4
$10 \leqslant t < 20$	14
$20 \leqslant t < 30$	4
$30 \leqslant t < 40$	1

Draw a suitable diagram to display the data.

24 A new medicine to cure the common cold is tested.

Eighty people are divided into two equal groups, A and B.

Only one of the groups is given the new medicine.

The time taken by the people in each group to overcome their cold is recorded.

Number of days to overcome cold	Group A frequencies	Group B frequencies
1	0	1
2	5	7
3	15	15
4	13	
5	7	

The doctor forgot to fill in the last **two** rows for Group B.

He says that the mean of both groups is the same.

Show clearly why the missing frequencies must be 3 and 14.

AQA Examination-style questions 🄺🄷

1 A student recorded the time, in minutes, that 50 people spent in the library.

Time, t (minutes)	Frequency
$0 < t \leqslant 10$	2
$10 < t \leqslant 20$	8
$20 < t \leqslant 30$	20
$30 < t \leqslant 40$	12
$40 < t \leqslant 50$	8

Calculate an estimate of the mean number of minutes spent in the library. *(4 marks)*

AQA 2008

2 David, Gareth and Kerry share out the contents of a jar of 600 sweets.

David receives $\frac{1}{4}$ of the sweets.

Gareth receives $\frac{5}{8}$ of the sweets.

What fraction of the sweets is left in the jar for Kerry?

(4 marks)

AQA 2007

3   Linda works at Shopsave.
She wonders if she would earn more working at Superspend.
Here is some information about Shopsave and Superspend.

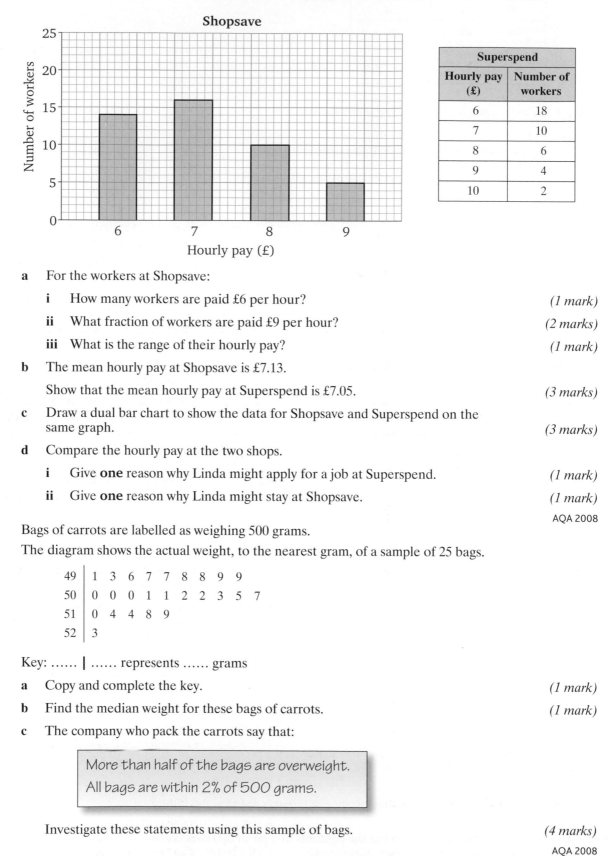

Shopsave

Superspend	
Hourly pay (£)	Number of workers
6	18
7	10
8	6
9	4
10	2

a   For the workers at Shopsave:

   i   How many workers are paid £6 per hour?   *(1 mark)*

   ii What fraction of workers are paid £9 per hour?   *(2 marks)*

   iii What is the range of their hourly pay?   *(1 mark)*

b   The mean hourly pay at Shopsave is £7.13.

   Show that the mean hourly pay at Superspend is £7.05.   *(3 marks)*

c   Draw a dual bar chart to show the data for Shopsave and Superspend on the
same graph.   *(3 marks)*

d   Compare the hourly pay at the two shops.

   i   Give **one** reason why Linda might apply for a job at Superspend.   *(1 mark)*

   ii Give **one** reason why Linda might stay at Shopsave.   *(1 mark)*

AQA 2008

4   Bags of carrots are labelled as weighing 500 grams.
The diagram shows the actual weight, to the nearest gram, of a sample of 25 bags.

```
49 | 1  3  6  7  7  8  8  9  9
50 | 0  0  0  1  1  2  2  3  5  7
51 | 0  4  4  8  9
52 | 3
```

Key: ...... | ...... represents ...... grams

a   Copy and complete the key.   *(1 mark)*

b   Find the median weight for these bags of carrots.   *(1 mark)*

c   The company who pack the carrots say that:

> More than half of the bags are overweight.
> All bags are within 2% of 500 grams.

   Investigate these statements using this sample of bags.   *(4 marks)*

AQA 2008

Glossary

amount – the principal + the interest (this is the total you will have in the bank, or the total you will owe the bank, at the end of the period of time).

average – the name given to a single value that represents a set of data.

back-to-back stem-and-leaf diagram – a stem-and-leaf diagram where the stem is down the centre and the leaves from two distributions are either side for comparison.

balance – how much money you have in your bank account.

bar chart – a frequency diagram where the height of a bar represents the frequency of an item.

biased – in the context of probability, not having the expected chance of happening.

certain – an outcome that has to happen.

class interval – the range of values within a group (class) of grouped data.

closed questions – questions that control the responses allowed by using option boxes.

composite bar chart – a frequency diagram for two or more sets of data with corresponding values from each set of data wholly contained within one bar.

continuous data – quantitative data that are measured but must be rounded to be recorded, such as heights, weights, times.

controlled experiment – data collection by a planned investigation of some type such as checking heart rates of runners.

coordinates – a system used to identify a point; an x-coordinate and a y-coordinate give the horizontal and vertical positions.

correlation – a measure of the relationship between two sets of data; correlation is measured in terms of type and strength.

credit – (i) when you buy goods 'on credit' you do not pay all the cost at once, instead you make a number of payments at regular intervals, often once a month; NB When your bank account is 'in credit', this means you have some money in it; (ii) how much you owe a shopkeeper after you have paid a deposit.

data collection sheet – prepared tables to record responses to questionnaires or outcomes for an observation such as noting car colours.

data logging – data collection by automatic machine such as in a shop entrance.

decimal – a number in which a decimal point separates the whole number part from the decimal part, for example, 17.46

decimal places – the number of digits to the right of the decimal point; e.g. the number 24.567 has three decimal places.

denominator – the number on the bottom of a fraction.

deposit – an amount of money you pay towards the cost of an item; the rest of the cost is paid later.

depreciation – a reduction in value (of used cars, for example).

digit – any of the numerals from 0 to 9.

directed number – a number with a direction (expressed by using a positive or negative sign) as well as a size; examples: $+3$, -0.3

discount – a reduction in the price; sometimes this is for paying in cash or paying early.

discrete data – quantitative data taking exact values such as frequencies, shoe size, dice scores.

dual bar chart – a multiple bar chart with specifically two sets of data.

equivalent fraction – two or more fractions that have the same value; Equivalent fractions can be made by multiplying or dividing the numerator and denominator of any fraction by the same number.

evens – the chance of an outcome that is equally likely to happen or not happen.

event – something that takes place that we want to find the probability of. For example, for finding the probability of 'getting an even number with one throw of a dice', the event is 'getting an even number with one throw of a dice'.

experimental probability – the chance of a particular outcome based on results of experiments or previous data.

fair – without bias; e.g. a fair coin has an equal chance of falling on head or tail.

frequency diagram – any chart or diagram which compares the frequencies of objects.

frequency polygon – a frequency diagram for continuous data with a line joining the midpoints of the class intervals using the appropriate frequencies.

frequency table – a table showing total number (frequency) against data values; like a tally chart but with a number instead of tallies.

grouped data – data that are separated into data classes.

histogram – a diagram for continuous data with bars as rectangles whose areas represent the frequency.

impossible – an outcome that cannot happen.

integer – any positive or negative whole number or zero, for example, -2, -1, 0, 1, 2, ...

interest – the money paid to you by a bank or building society when you save your money in an account with them; (it is also the money you pay for borrowing from a bank!).

key – an indication of how many items a symbol in a pictogram represents or which type of shading represents which data in other diagrams.

likely – an outcome that probably will happen.

line graph – a diagram for continuous data, usually over a period of time.

line of best fit – a line drawn to represent the relationship between two sets of data; ideally it should only be drawn where the correlation is strong, for example:

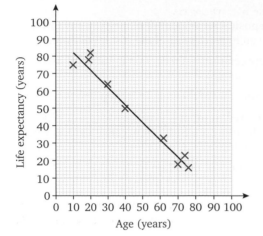

mean – the total of all the values divided by the number of values (also called the arithmetic mean).

$$\text{Mean} = \frac{\text{the total of (frequencies} \times \text{values)}}{\text{the total of frequencies}} = \frac{\Sigma fx}{\Sigma f}$$

median – the middle value when the data are listed in order.

mixed number – a fraction that has both a whole number and a fraction part.

modal class or modal group – the class or group within a frequency table that occurs most often.

mode – the value or item that occurs most often.

mutually exclusive events – events that are mutually exclusive cannot happen.

natural (counting) number – a number normally used for counting; a positive integer; examples: 1, 2, 3 …

negative correlation – as one set of data increase, the other set of data decreases.

negative number – a number less than zero, expressed with a negative sign; examples: −5.3, −400

numerator – the number on the top of a fraction.

observation – data collection by watching something happen.

observation sheet – prepared tables to record responses to questionnaires or outcomes for an observation such as noting car colours.

open questions – allow for any response to be made by using an answer space.

outcome – one of the possible results of an experiment or trial. For example, when rolling a dice there are six possible outcomes: 1, 2, 3, 4, 5, 6

outlier – a value that does not fit the general trend, for example:

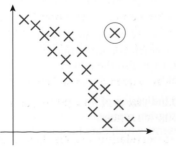

percentage – the number of parts per hundred; for example, 9% means '9 out of 100' or $\frac{9}{100}$

pictogram – a pictogram uses symbols to represent items of data.

pie chart – a frequency diagram where the angle of a sector represents the frequency of an item.

pilot survey – a small scale survey carried out before the main survey.

population – every possible item that could occur in a given situation.

positive correlation – as one set of data increases, the other set of data increases.

positive number – a number greater than zero; sometimes expressed with a positive sign; examples: +18.3, 0.36

primary data – data you have collected yourself, usually for a specific purpose.

principal – the money put into the bank (or borrowed from the bank).

probability – a measure of how likely an event is to occur.

probability scale – a scale running from 0 to 1 on which events can be placed to indicate how likely they are to occur.

proportion – compares one part with the whole, whereas a ratio compares one part with another; if a class has 10 boys and 15 girls, the proportion of boys in the class is $\frac{10}{25}$ (which simplifies to $\frac{2}{5}$), the proportion of girls in the class is $\frac{15}{25}$ (which simplifies to $\frac{3}{5}$).

qualitative data – data that cannot be measured using numbers, e.g. hair colour, sports, breeds of sheep.

quantitative data – data that can be measured or counted such as heights, ages, times, frequencies.

questionnaire – data collection by a series of questions requiring responses.

range – the difference between the highest value and the lowest value in a distribution (a measure of spread, not a measure of average).

rate – the percentage at which interest is added.

ratio – a means of comparing numbers or quantities; a ratio shows how much bigger one number or quantity is than another; if two numbers or quantities are in the ratio 1 : 2, the second is always twice as big as the first; if two numbers or quantities are in the ratio 2 : 5, for every 2 parts of the first there are 5 parts of the second.

raw data – data before they have been sorted in any way.

relative frequency – the fraction or proportion of the number of times out of the total that a particular outcome occurs.

round – give an approximate value of a number; numbers can be rounded to the nearest 1000, nearest 100, nearest 10, nearest integer, significant figures, decimal places, …, etc.

sample – a small part of a population from which information is taken.

sample size – the number of people or items in the sample.

sample space diagram – a table or diagram showing all possible outcomes for an event.

scatter graph – a graph used to show the relationship between two sets of variables, for example, temperature and ice cream sales:

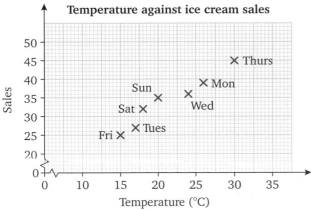

Temperature against ice cream sales

secondary data – data that others have collected; anything from newspapers, the internet and similar sources.

significant figures – the digits in a number; the closer a digit is to the beginning of a number then the more important or significant it is; for example, in the number 23.657, 2 is the most significant digit and is worth 20, 7 is the least significant digit and is worth 7 units; the number 23.657 has 5 significant digits.

stem-and-leaf diagram – a frequency diagram which uses the actual values of the data split into a stem and leaves; the diagram needs a key.

strength of correlation – the strength of correlation is an indication of how close the points lie to a straight line (perfect correlation); correlation is usually described in terms of strong correlation, weak correlation or no correlation.

Strong correlation

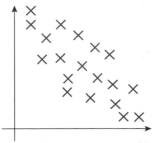

Weak correlation

survey – general name for data collection using interviews or questionnaires.

tally chart – a method of organising raw data into a table using a five bar gate method of tallying.

theoretical probability – the chance of a particular outcome based on equally likely outcomes.

time – is measured in years to work out interest (per annum means per year).

trial – a probability experiment consisting of a number of individual trials. For example, if an experiment is 'throw a dice' and it is thrown 20 times, then that is 20 trials.

two-way table – a table showing information about two sets of data at the same time.

type of correlation –

Positive correlation

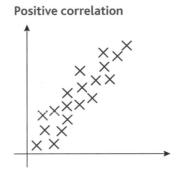

in positive correlation an increase in one set of variables results in an increase in the other set of variables;

Negative correlation

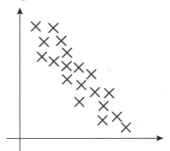

in negative correlation an increase in one set of variables results in a decrease in the other set of variables;

Zero correlation

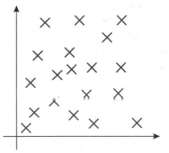

zero or no correlation is where there is no obvious relationship between the two sets of data.

unitary method – a method of calculating quantities that are in proportion by first finding one unit; for example, if 12 litres of petrol cost £11.76 you can find the cost of 10 litres:

12 litres cost   £11.76
1 litre costs   £11.76 ÷ 12 = £0.98
10 litres costs   £0.98 × 10 = £9.80

unitary ratio – a ratio in the form $1 : n$ or $n : 1$; this form of ratio is helpful for comparison, as it shows clearly how much of one quantity there is for one unit of the other.

unlikely – an outcome that probably will not happen.

Value Added Tax (V.A.T.) – this tax is added on to the price of goods or services.

zero or no correlation – where there is no obvious relationship between the two sets of data.

Index

A
adding
    decimals   26–7
    directed numbers   8
    fractions   12
amount   48
assess   21–2, 30–1, 43–4, 59–60, 69–70, 81–2, 96–8, 110–11, 125–6
averages   **71, 72,** 74
    see also mean, median, mode

B
back-to-back stem-and-leaf diagrams   **91,** 92
balance   54
bar charts   84–6
bias (surveys)   38
biased dice   121

C
calculators
    keys   47, 51, 62
    using   8, 29, 47
card packs   115
certain   113
class interval   41, **78,** 79, 93
closed questions   **36**
coins, fair   113
combining events   116
composite bar charts   **85,** 86
consolidation   127–36
continuous data   **33, 78,** 89, 128
    grouped   93
controlled experiments   **37**
coordinate points   **101**
correlation   103–4
    strength of   104
    zero or none   102, **103,** 105
counting numbers   8
credit   54

D
data collection
    methods   36–7
    sheet (observation sheet)   **40**
data-handling cycle   33
data logging   **37**
data sets   72, 74, 89
    comparing   85
data types   33
decimal multiplier   49, 50, 51, 52
decimal place   **25**
decimal points   24
decimals   **12**
    adding   26–7
    and fractions, comparing   47
    to fractions   29
    multiplying   28
    negative   11, 12
    to percentages   47, 54
    subtracting   26–7
denominator   14, 17, **29**
deposit   54
depreciation   52
dice, fair   113, 121–2
digits   24
directed numbers   8, 10–11

discount   53
discrete data   **33,** 78, 89
    quantitative   84
dividing integers   11
dual bar charts   **85**

E
equivalent fractions   **14**
estimating answers   27, 28
evens   **113**
events   **113,** 114, 118–19
    combining   116
    mutually exclusive   **118-19**
experimental probability (relative frequency)   **121–2**
experiments, controlled   **37**

F
fair coins and dice   **113, 121–2**
formulae
    for mean   74, 75, 78, 79
    probability   114, 118, 121
fraction grids   16
fraction wall diagrams   15, 16
fractions   12
    adding   12
    and decimals, comparing   47
    to decimals   17, 29
    equivalent   **14**
    multiplying   12
    in music   7
    negative   11, 12
    arranging in order   17
    to percentages   47, 54
    of quantities   18, 19
    simplifying   29, 62
frequency   78
frequency diagrams   **93,** 128
frequency distributions   74–5
    grouped   78–9
frequency polygons   **93,** 128
frequency tables   **39,** 74, 75
    grouped   79
fuel prices   20

G
glossary   137–9
graphs, line   **92–3**
grouped data   **78,** 79
    continuous   93
grouped frequency distributions   78–9

H
histograms   **93,** 94
horizontal (*x*-) axis   84, 100, 101
hundredths   24, 29
hypothesis   **33**

I
impossible   **113**
insurance   112
integers (whole numbers)   **8,** 24
    dividing   11
    multiplying   10–11
interest   **54**
interviews   37

K
key 84, 91

L
likely 113
line graphs 92–3
lines of best fit 107–8

M
map scales 64
mean 72, 74, 75, 78
    estimated 79
median 72, 74, 75, 78, 79
mixed numbers 12
modal class (modal group) 78, 79
mode 72, 74, 75, 78
multiplying
    decimals 28
    fractions 12
    integers 10–11
music notes 7, 13
mutually exclusive events 118–19

N
natural (counting) numbers 8
negative correlation 103, 104
negative numbers 8, 10–11
number lines 8, 12, 14, 25
numerator 14, 17, 29

O
observation 37
observation (data collection) sheet 40
open questions 36
organising data 39–41
outcome 113, 114
outliers (rogue values) 104, 107

P
percentages 47
    increase and decrease 51, 57
    profit and loss 57
    of a quantity 49, 54–5
pictograms 84, 87
pie charts 83, 86–7
pilot surveys 36
place value 24
place value table 29
plotting points 99
population 34
positive correlation 103, 104
positive numbers 8, 10–11
primary data 33
principal 52
probability 113–14
    combining events 116
    experimental (relative frequency) 121–2
    mutually exclusive outcomes 118–19
    theoretical 113–14, 116, 118–19, **121, 122**
probability scales 113
proportion 62
    unitary method 66

Q
qualitative data 33, 84
quantitative data 33, 84
questionnaires 36–7

questions, exam-style 22, 31, 45, 60, 70, 82, 98, 111, 126, 135
questions, open and closed 36

R
range 72, 74, 75, 78, 90
rate 51
ratio 61, 62–3
    to find quantities 64–5
    unitary method 66
raw data 33, 39
relative frequency (experimental probability) 121–2
    graph 122
rounding 25, 28

S
sample 34
sample size 34
sample space diagrams 116
scale on graphs 84, 100
scales on maps 64
scatter graphs (diagrams) 99, 100–1, 107–8
    interpreting 103–4
    plotting points 100
secondary data 33
significant figures 24, 25, 29
simplest form 29, 62
sorting numbers 24
spinners 123, 129
spread 72, 74
stem-and-leaf diagrams 89–91
    back-to-back 91, 92
strength of correlation 104
subtracting
    decimals 26–7
    directed numbers 8
surveys 36–7
    pilot 36

T
tally charts 39, 40
tens 24
tenths 24
theoretical probability 113–14, 116, 118–19, **121, 122**
thermometers 8
thousandths 24, 29
trials 121
two-way tables 40, 116
types of correlation 103–4

U
unitary method 66
unitary ratio 64
units 24
unlikely 113

V
Value Added Tax (VAT) 50, 51
vertical (y-) axis 84, 100

W
whole numbers (integers) 8, 10–11, 24

Z
zero or no correlation 102, 103, 105
zeros 25, 27